Meet the Stars of

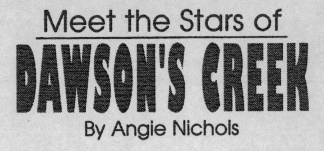

DAWSON'S CREEK

By Angie Nichols

D0827689

SCHOLASTIC INC.
New York Toronto London Auckland Sydney

ISBN 0-590-64269-3

12 11 10 9 8 7 6 5   8 9/9 0 1 2 3/0

Printed in the U.S.A.

First Scholastic printing, June 1998

This book could not have been written without the faith and guidance of my editor, who has been a great teacher and an inspiration in more ways then she'll ever realize. Thank you!

Contents

Chapter 1: Welcome to *Dawson's Creek*   1

Chapter 2: Meet James   12

Chapter 3: Say Hi to Katie   31

Chapter 4: It's Josh   47

Chapter 5: Hanging With Michelle   64

Chapter 6: Raves and Waves   83

Chapter 7: Just the Facts   93

Chapter 8: It's All in the Stars   117

Chapter 9: Predictions, Where to Write, and More!   128

1

Welcome to *Dawson's Creek*

"It was the end of something simple. And the beginning of everything else."

Being fifteen has never been easy. It's an age that straddles the cusp between childhood and adulthood — who we are today and who we'll be tomorrow morning. In past generations, people at fifteen were still kids; they didn't have the choices and the freedom that teenagers do today. That freedom can bring about once-in-a-lifetime happiness, like first kisses and lazy days with friends chasing seagulls along a windswept beach, but it can also bring about heartache and sadness. For better or worse, the choices someone makes today at fifteen can completely change the path his or her life takes forever.

Real teenage life, in all its scariness and breathless excitement, is exactly what *Dawson's Creek* is all about!

The first joyous notes of Paula Cole's hit single "I Don't Want to Wait" playing over the show's opening credits announce that *Dawson's Creek* is special. Set in the gorgeous fictional town of Capeside, a place that could be in any seaside part of the country, the show focuses on the lives of four fifteen-year-olds as they try to figure out who they are and where they fit in. There's Pacey, the sarcastic wisecracking goof, and Jen, the girl from New York City, who's just trying to find her place. Joey is the tomboy with a crush on her best friend. And, of course, there's Dawson, the film-obsessed dreamer who lives in his own little world, where he imagines becoming Hollywood's next great film director. Together, these four are wise beyond their years in the ways of the world but completely hopeless when it comes to matters of the heart.

"I think people can really relate to the show," said series star James Van Der Beek to *Teen Machine* magazine. "I think there's an element of fantasy of, 'I wish I grew up like that.' It's just a small little town and I think it will be nice for people to just sort of curl up and watch and enjoy."

These Friends of Mine

And that's exactly what millions of people did on January 13, 1998, when the WB TV network introduced the world to the captivating cast of *Dawson's Creek*. As Dawson Leery, movie-crazed high school sophomore and video store clerk on weekdays, and producer/director of *Sea Serpent from the Deep* on weekends, James touched audiences with his combination of innocent enthusiasm and swaggering confidence. Movies are Dawson's life. He believes that "all of life's answers can be found in a Spielberg film." His friends accuse him of having the "perfect" life, but Dawson's just starting to discover that people are never as flawless in real life as they are in the movies. That goes double for his "perfect" parents, whose relationship turned out to have some major problems.

Two of the greatest influences of Dawson's life are his best pals: Joey Potter, played by Hollywood newcomer Katie Holmes, and cutup Pacey Witter, played nimbly by *Mighty Ducks* movie veteran Joshua Jackson.

One of the first shocks to Dawson's blissful existence is Joey's sudden assertion that it's just not a good idea for her to sleep over at his house anymore. Although she's slept over since they were seven, they're not little kids anymore, she reasons, and sooner or later an inevitable romantic moment will come along and ruin their perfect friendship. Later on, of course, the wisdom of Joey's decision finally dawns on Dawson.

To Joey, Dawson's friendship is one of the most important ties in her life. Her own family is so fragmented, and Dawson's friendship has given her substantial stability. Joey lives with her older sister, Bessie, Bessie's new baby, and Bessie's boyfriend, Bodie, in a small house where privacy is non-existent. Joey silently mourns her mother, who died of cancer not long ago. Her father, meanwhile, is serving jail time on a drug rap. Joey's often the target of gossip at school. Through it all, this tough girl just digs in her heels. When she needs a break from real life, she climbs the ladder to Dawson's room. "It's one of those really strong bonds, but neither one of them are quite sure exactly where it lies," explained James of the relationship between Joey and Dawson to the cable network, E!

Dawson's other best friend is class clown Pacey Witter. With a father who is Capeside's police chief and a by-the-rule brother, Doug, who is also a cop, Pacey's been told by his family that he's a loser so many times he's starting to believe it himself. So he goofs off in school and maintains a less-than-brilliant C average. The other students at Capeside High laugh *at* him more than they laugh *with* him. But Dawson and Joey stand by his side because he's a loyal friend. He'd do anything for Dawson and the other people he cares about. And the truth is, at heart, Pacey is honorable and usually ends up doing the right thing.

As much as he loves his friends, nobody touched Dawson's heart more than his new next-door neighbor, gorgeous blond Jennifer Lindley, played by Michelle Williams. Dawson was immediately attracted to the beautiful and mysterious Jen the minute he saw her. Shot with a rack of Cupid's arrows, he created an elaborate fantasy about who Jen was and what she would become to him. Unfortunately, it had absolutely no basis in reality.

Jen was never a bad person, nor was she the angel Dawson believed her to be. Although she told her new friends that she'd come to Capeside to help her grandmother nurse her grandfather back to health, the truth turned out to be much more complicated. As Jen eventually blurted out to Dawson, "You know what they say about city kids being wild and growing up too soon? I *was* those kids." Her parents, finally fed up with her party-girl escapades, sent her to live with her super-religious grandmother in a quiet little town in hopes that she'd regain some innocence. Jen wasn't looking for a serious romantic relationship when she arrived. She just wanted to make friends, be happy, and slow down enough to discover who she really is.

A Different Kind of Show

Neither as depressing as *Party of Five*, nor as gushy as the lightweight *Beverly Hills, 90210*, *Dawson's Creek* is a tantalizing drama sprinkled liberally with a fresh dose of laughter. Although the fictional town of Capeside is supposed to be located just outside of Boston, it has the feel of any small seaside town. Everyone knows each other and neighbors feel at liberty to share words of wisdom uninvited. Plus, Capeside, with its dramatic sunsets and its creek that flows lazily through Dawson's backyard, is a beautiful place to spend an hour each week no matter where you really live.

Like the location, the characters who populate Dawson's world are easy to relate to and even easier to love. After all, who hasn't known a funny class clown like Pacey whose jokes mask his insecurities? And new kids, especially the ones like Jen who come from a far-off city, are always regarded with curiosity and often a bit of suspicion. Joey, meanwhile, is the tough girl who makes cutting remarks in hopes of hiding her broken heart. She's so afraid to admit weakness that she lets very few people know what she's feeling inside. And then there's Dawson, who's a bit of a dreamer and a lot more naive than his friends but who somehow manages to hold the people he loves around him like some bright shining sun. Maybe it is just his ability to dream that transports his friends away from the difficult reality of their own lives and into the warm glow of his own.

Based on a True Story

From where did the spark for these familiar characters come? Well, writer and series creator Kevin Williamson (the guy who wrote the hip *Scream* movies and *I Know What You Did Last Summer*) admits that many of the fictional Capeside residents are based on real people he knew growing up. In fact, Kevin cops to being the model for Dawson.

Like his golden-haired alter ego, Kevin also grew up worshipping the movies. Dawson idolizes filmmaker Steven Spielberg, while Kevin confesses it was the teen-oriented films of John Hughes, like *The Breakfast Club*, *Pretty in Pink*, and *Sixteen Candles*, that made him want to become a filmmaker or an actor. A critical high school teacher told him not to bother with acting. He had no talent. Unfortunately, after several unsuccessful years as a wannabe actor, it looked like she was right.

But a funny thing happened on the way to acting obscurity. Kevin became inspired to write — and after many moderate successes, the screenplay for the movie *Scream* came out of his computer. Suddenly, Kevin was A-list cool in Hollywood.

Kevin followed up *Scream* by writing two sequels to the hit movie, as well as the script for *I Know What You Did Last Summer*, an adaptation of the popular young adult thriller by Lois Duncan. But after all the thrills and chills, he landed in *Dawson's Creek*. "I had no more scary stories to tell, so I reached into my childhood and came up with — me," admitted Kevin to E! online. "It's this young kid in a small town who wants to be a filmmaker. He loves Spielberg, has a crush on the girl next door, and his best friend of fifteen years is secretly longing for him. I pitched it as *Some Kind of Wonderful* meets *Pump Up the Volume* meets *James at 15* meets *My So-Called Life* meets *Little House on the Prairie*. I sort of threw everything in there."

Although not everything that happens on *Dawson's Creek* happened to Kevin in real life, a lot of it did. When he was in high school, a student really fell in love with his teacher, much like Pacey's doomed relationship with English teacher Tamara Jacobs. Kevin and his friends also filmed their own swamp creature movie, like Dawson's *Sea Serpent from the Deep* starring Pacey in a green monster costume and Joey and Jen as his victims. Kevin also had a platonic pal who was a girl. "I had that best friend, Joey — in real life her name was Fanny. We were best friends all the way through high school," he explained to E! "I just talked to her recently for the first time in about ten years. She had no idea I'd writ-

9

ten *Scream*. She was like, 'You know, there's a writer out there with your name, Kevin. He wrote *Scream*.'" And while it looks like Dawson and Joey will become much more than just friends, it's interesting to also know that for a couple of years in college, Kevin and Fanny actually did date each other!

Although Kevin grew up in North Carolina — not too far from the city of Wilmington, where the show is actually filmed — he remembers his coastal town having a New England flavor to it because of all the transplanted Northerners there. In naming the show, he paid tribute to one of his favorite hometown hangout spots — the real Dawson's Creek. He fondly explained, "[The creek] holds this special memory for me."

Something Special

The cast members who bring to life Dawson Leery, Pacey Witter, Joey Potter, and Jen Lindley agree that *Dawson's Creek* holds a special place in their hearts, too. Although it's not the first drama series to explore the teen years, it's doing it in a different way than *Party of Five*, *Beverly Hills, 90210*, or even the critically acclaimed *My So-Called Life*.

"*Dawson's Creek* is much more about friend-

10

ships and redefining your friendships — going through those really intense, painful years," said Joshua Jackson to *Tiger Beat* magazine. "Of course, I'm a little biased, but I would watch it because it's a good show. I think it's a good portrayal of teen life and it's a pretty honest show. We deal with issues that are pertinent in the average teenager's life ... and I think that's what is making the show so successful."

James, too, praises *Dawson's Creek* for its openness about teenagers' real-life concerns. "I think our show is honest, and I'm not ashamed of anything that happens on it," he said during an online chat with E! "The content is so mild compared with trashy talk shows that are on at three in the afternoon, and we deal so much more intelligently and responsibly with these issues than anyone on those shows ever does."

Creator Kevin Williamson adds that critics who frown at the frankness of the dialogue on the show are completely missing what *Dawson's Creek* is all about. "It's about hand holding and sweaty palms and that first kiss," he explained in an interview with the *Shawnee News-Star*. "The show is meant to be touching, bittersweet, and romantic and funny."

11

2
Meet James

Because Dawson Leery is the central character, it was critical to find the right actor to portray him. He had to have a genuine boy-next-door quality with the right balance of fresh-faced enthusiasm and '90s self-awareness. He couldn't be too hip, but he couldn't be a complete nerd, either. This actor needed to be virtually unknown, but he also needed enough talent and experience to carry the show. After all, Dawson is in practically every scene!

The strong buzz in Hollywood about the new series from the writer of *Scream* gave Kevin a wealth of young actors from which to choose. In fact, his production company was flooded with resumés, photographs, letters, and videotapes from practically every young hopeful between the ages of fifteen and twenty-five! It was a difficult job. Kevin and the other producers of the series hired all three other major actors — Josh Jackson as Pacey, Katie Holmes as Joey, and Michelle Williams as Jen — before they were able to agree on their series star.

James Van Der Beek, a then nineteen-year-old actor and college student with a lot of theater experience, two TV appearances (on *Clarissa Explains It All* and an after-school special), and a few movie roles on his resumé, was sent to the *Dawson's Creek* audition by his agent. A junior on an academic scholarship at New Jersey's prestigious Drew University, James had to miss classes and take the train to New York during the middle of the afternoon to try out for the role. It was a situation, he admits, that annoyed him at the time. When the producers asked him to fly out to Los Angeles later that week for yet another audition, this time with Kevin Williamson, he reacted with less than one hundred percent enthusiasm. He promised that he'd see what he could do. But minutes later, as he sat reading the complete *Daw-*

son's Creek script in New York's Penn Station terminal while waiting for a train back to school, James's annoyance quickly turned to fear that he'd blown his chance. "It made me nervous because I suddenly realized that I *wanted* to do this," he told the *Chicago Tribune*. "The honesty, the intelligence — *Dawson's Creek* was quite different from anything I had read this season."

James dropped everything and made arrangements to travel to Los Angeles. He also prepared for meeting Kevin by renting *Scream*, a movie he'd missed seeing due to his busy college schedule. What a mistake! After watching the hit thriller he was *more* nervous than ever! What would it be like to be face-to-face with the brilliant writer who had created such a twisted tale of suspense and murder?

Luckily, James had nothing to worry about. When Kevin welcomed him with a warm handshake, the producer's khaki pants, Polo shirt, and docksiders reminded James of many of the young professors he'd had at Drew University. His first impression was that the thirty-two-year-old writer was very down-to-earth and cool. He was even more impressed when Kevin, after learning that the young college student was planning to rent a hotel room he could scarcely afford, offered to let him crash on his couch. "Kevin is great," James told E! online. "He's one of the nicest, most humble people I've met in this business." Merely three days after this meeting with Kevin, James nailed the part. He swiftly withdrew from his classes and flew down to the North Carolina set of *Dawson's Creek* to begin filming the series pilot.

"Some people may want to kill me after they hear this, but *Dawson's* is the first pilot I ever filmed, the first I ever auditioned for," James told a reporter from the *Orange County Register.* "This is an opportunity that comes along maybe once."

Daydream Believer

"I call Dawson the dork in all of us," James said in an interview with New York's *Newsday.* "He's not really, really cool, and he's not part of the 'in' crowd. He's, you know, different. And I think a lot of the things he goes through are universal."

Dreamy Dawson Leery prefers to live in his own imagination. "I reject reality," he once said to his best friend Joey. With a warm smile, he trips through his life like it's one long Technicolor movie with a very happy ending. An idealist, Dawson can't help but look for the good in others. Though he's often let down by the people he loves, he doesn't really know how to hold a grudge. He's often blind to other people's troubles, making him seem insensitive sometimes, but when confronted, he's quick to realize his oversight and apologize. Living in his own little world populated by his happy fantasies, he's completely unaware of real life — until it comes crashing down on him!

"I definitely relate to my character," James said to E! "He's a lot like I was at fifteen — innocent, idealistic, impassioned, and often clueless." James admits that as a teenager he was also every bit as ambitious as his character. "Dawson and I were both very impassioned at an early age," explained James to *Teen Machine*. "Dawson is a burgeoning filmmaker, whose overactive imagination and idealism sometimes make him oblivious. He is prone to rejecting reality for a more romantic scenario. He's a bit of an innocent and is frequently off in his own little world, all of which I can definitely relate to. And we both come from loving, supportive homes." But Dawson is in for some surprises. James told the *Chicago Tribune*, "His ideal little world is going to dissolve around him, and he's going to have to deal with it."

James, who hails from Cheshire, Connecticut, spent his childhood in an environment almost as pretty as Capeside. "I grew up in a small New England town and vacationed on Cape Cod, where the show takes place," he said to a television reporter.

When James entered the freshman class at Cheshire Academy, he claims he was every bit as naive as Dawson. "I identify with his innocence a little bit. When I was sixteen, I was at a private school and was kind of blown away by what I was seeing," he admitted.

A Perfect Life

"Accept your perfect life, Dawson," Joey once said. "It's a reality." Off-screen, James could be accused of having a perfect life, too!

James, whose last name is Dutch for "by the brook," is from a happy family that includes a mom and dad who are still together, as well as a younger brother and sister. Growing up in Cheshire, which is located slightly southwest of the center of the state, James played a lot of sports. The son of a former minor league baseball player dad and former dancer mom, he excelled at baseball and gymnastics. From earliest childhood, he loved to climb the highest tree or show off his back flip from the diving board of the community pool. He never even considered acting. "It was funny," he told *Teen Machine*. "In eighth grade we were asked to write a letter to ourselves about where we would be in five years. I wrote that I either wanted to be a pro baseball player like my father or I wanted to be a physical therapist. Acting wasn't anywhere near my mind."

But athletics was not to be. Because of a mild concussion during the autumn he turned thirteen, James was ordered by his doctor not to try out for the football team. He needed to find another activity to fill up the fall months, so he tried out for the school play. Much to everyone's surprise, James walked away with the lead role of Danny Zuko in the musical *Grease*.

The thrill of performing in front of a live audience hooked James on acting. Luckily, he was able to hone his skill right in Cheshire at the community theater. "I was introduced to a couple of musicals that I really loved, like *Jesus Christ Superstar* and things like that

that really blew me away," he recalled to *16* magazine. "I started listening to sound tracks and then there came a point where I said, 'I can do that!'"

By age sixteen, acting had become a major passion for James, despite a discouraging drama teacher at Cheshire Academy who told him that he didn't have the talent for anything more challenging than community theater. Wounded by those harsh remarks, James was even more determined to make it outside of his hometown. His mom was understanding and volunteered to help.

"My mother saw my intense interest and said, 'If this is something you really want to try, I'll take you to New York for the summer,'" James shared in *USA Today*. Although he found an agent and a manager on the first day, success didn't happen overnight. "My agent sent me out on commercials, which I cannot book to save my life," he explained. "Even when I was really poor in college and praying, 'Oh, please, let me get this,' I need the money — I never did."

What went wrong? "I just think I took those auditions really seriously," James theorized to *Totally TV*. "I only got one in my entire career, and it was something I was totally wrong for. It was for Oxy [acne cream]. I was totally broken out, but I was supposed to be the guy with the clear skin, so they had to totally cover me with makeup!"

A less driven actor might have given up, but after a year and a half of disheartening auditions James's persistence finally paid off. He nailed his first job on the New York stage.

Off-Broadway Bound

Finding the Sun is a play written and directed by three-time Pulitzer Prize-winning playwright Edward Albee. Although at seventeen James was still in high school, he tried out for the play and won a key role. It was a demanding job. For the three months of rehearsals and performances James commuted six hours back and forth to New York City every day. "That was an amazing experience." James recalled to *16* magazine. "It really helped shape my career. We got a nice write-up in *The New York Times* and I sent that around with my head shot to casting directors."

James's next career highlight was the lead in *Shenandoah* at the Goodspeed Opera House. This show presented a different challenge for the teenager. "In *Shenandoah*, I had to dance," he said to *Tiger Beat* magazine. "I am by no means a dancer. But actually, what they [were] looking for was a more athletic type of dancer — not so much ballet." Luckily, James's experience as a gymnast made it pretty easy to master the *Shenandoah* dance routines.

Shenandoah was a good experience for James, but he was disappointed when the show's three-month run at Goodspeed was not followed by an engagement on Broadway. "There was talk that it might make it to Broadway, but there was a problem," he explained to *Tiger Beat*. "It was a very talented cast but we didn't get great reviews. For something to make its way to Broadway, you really need raves."

Movie Mania

Not long after his high school graduation, James landed his first movie role in the 1995 film *Angus*. A generic coming-of-age story, *Angus* is the tale of an overweight teenager's fight for acceptance at school and in his own heart. In the movie, James plays Angus's archenemy, Rick Sanford, a blond-haired bully of a football player.

James, who was still appearing nightly in *Shenandoah*, rushed to his *Angus* audition without reading the script. In creating the character, he simply based his performance on a bully who used to pick on *him* at school! "I kind of used one person who used to give me a lot of flak in middle school," James said during a *16* magazine interview. "He plays on my brother's football team. After I knew I got the part, I ran into him and just kind of laughed at him, 'Look at this, I got a feature film because of all the stuff you did to me!'" For James, winning that job was the sweetest revenge of all.

After *Angus*, James played the part of yet another bully in the film *I Love You . . . I Love You Not*, which starred Claire Danes. As Tony, James is particularly awful to Claire's character. "I play another despicable character," he said to *Tiger Beat*. "She plays a very sweet girl and I play this evil guy. I'm awful, terrible to her."

The premiere of *I Love You . . . I Love You Not* ended up being delayed for more than two years. Still, the lessons James learned from Claire about dealing with fame would come in handy in his near future. "She's just a very sweet girl — incredibly talented," James told *16*. He was impressed by how at ease she was when talking with her young fans, who often confused her with *My So-Called Life*'s Angela Chase. "She would walk to the set from her trailer followed like the Pied Piper by hordes of pubescent girls," he recalled. "They didn't ask for an autograph, they just wanted to walk alongside her. Watching that, I was like, 'How is this girl keeping sane?'" Of course, James soon would find out how to deal with fans himself!

School Stuff

As fate would have it, neither movie turned out to be James's big break. *Angus* faded away pretty quickly at the box office, while *I Love You . . . I Love You Not* lingered unreleased on the film studio's shelf. In the meantime, the stage remained a big passion for him. As recently as 1997, he appeared in the off-Broadway play *My Marriage to Ernest Borgnine*. He also filmed a role in the independent feature *Harvest*, a movie about a group of down-on-their-luck farmers who decide to start growing a new, very illegal substance. But as few roles came his way, James became a bit discouraged. He even briefly considered giving up acting altogether.

However, the break from work gave James the opportunity to experience all the fun of college life. He lived on campus, attended parties with his circle of friends, and threw himself into his studies. Though his heart was always set on acting, his family had impressed upon him the importance of a well-rounded education. "I'm going to study everything other than theater," James said to *Tiger Beat* the summer before his freshman year. "I figure the more you have at your disposal, the better."

Since he loved reading and writing from early childhood, he settled on a major in English with a minor in sociology. If acting didn't work out, he wanted to be prepared for another career. "I'd probably be a teacher — a middle school teacher. I had a real mentor from middle school, and it's such a miserable time for any kid," he said during an online chat at Ultimate TV about his backup plans. In fact, James's love of classic literature would have made him a great English teacher. His favorite book is James Joyce's *Portrait of the Artist as a Young Man*. "It's more a study in metaphor than a page-turning story, but I really identified with Stephen Daedalus. It was fascinating to watch him stumble his way to his true passion, having already discovered mine," he said to E! online.

Although James left college to take the role on *Dawson's Creek*, he plans to go back and finish his degree someday. "I'm actually a semester and four credits ahead. I took a leave of absence but I definitely plan on going back," explained this college junior during his Ultimate TV online interview.

On *Dawson's Creek*

In August 1997, the four stars of *Dawson's Creek* reported to the set in Wilmington, North Carolina, to begin filming the first season. Since none of them knew anyone else in town, they hung out together a lot. They spent time shopping in downtown Wilmington, going to the movies, or having dinner together at their favorite eatery, The Deluxe, a restaurant downstairs from James and Josh's apartment. "It's really cool, the other cast members are great. We're isolated in North Carolina and not caught up in Hollywood. We've all become really good friends, too," James raved to a reporter.

Dawson's Creek's two male stars actually shared an apartment during the first season, while Katie and Michelle lived only blocks away. Although they are good friends, James has questioned the wisdom of sharing living space with one of his costars. "The other day I was like, 'How stupid were we?'" James told a writer from *Seventeen* magazine. "Fortunately, we've managed not to kill each other. We get along well."

Tucked away in a sleepy town far from the bright lights of Hollywood, James and the other actors could concentrate on their work, rather than the fame the job would bring. "Wilmington is actually a really great town. We hang out, go out with the crew, go out with the cast, go to the beach," James said in the same *Seventeen* interview. "I'm so glad I'm not in L.A. right now. It would kill me. Doing a series is so much of a head trip as it is."

Hollywood Awaits

When *Dawson's Creek* finally aired in January 1998, James and the rest of the cast flew to Los Angeles and New Orleans to meet the press — and the show's new fans. "It's funny . . . being in the show was our day-to-day reality," James said during an online chat. "Now it's getting weird. Fortunately, the distraction came after the work."

That distraction included a group of young *Dawson's Creek* fans competing to get near James and Josh at a magazine party. "We walked out and everybody went nuts," James told *USA Today*. "We were throwing T-shirts out to the fans but we had to stop because people were trampling each other to get them."

Because he plays Dawson, James has received the lion's share of interview and personal appearance requests. His solo promotional trip to Seattle, Washington, was a shock to this serious young actor. "There were five thousand screaming teenage girls going, 'Oh, my God, you rock! You're hot! I love you!'" he told *Entertainment Weekly*. James admits he is uncomfortable with all the attention. "I've never felt more detached from a group of people in my life. I was like a deer in the headlights. I didn't know how to react!"

Fame is something James is still having a hard time getting used to. He was quoted in *Entertainment Weekly* saying he didn't look forward to appearing on the cover of teen magazines. He's an actor because he loves the work, not because he's hungry for fame. "It was taken a little bit out of context," he said later about the *EW* quote. "They asked me if I was excited about that. I said . . . it's not why I started acting." He added in another online interview, "It's quite strange. Flattering and exciting, but strange. I always feel so detached from the people who recognize me, because they know the Dawson persona. They don't know *me* at all. I'd be lying if I said I didn't think it was pretty cool, but I'm never quite sure how to react."

James is naturally thrilled that people like *Dawson's Creek*, but he's mostly excited about the work he's done on the show. "I'd just rather do good work," he said to a reporter from the *Shawnee News-Star.* "If people see it, that would be icing on the cake." He said he would prefer to star on "a good show that nobody watches than a bad show that's wildly popular but something that I'm not proud of."

Time Out

The hectic schedule James and his costars have gotten used to in filming *Dawson's Creek* leaves very little time for hobbies or even dating. The cast and crew often have dinner together in one of the many restaurants in downtown Wilmington. On days off, James likes to take advantage of the North Carolina location and visit one of the many gorgeous beaches within easy driving distance. "It's not a huge culture shock," said James to *Tiger Beat.* Facetiously, he added, "I think there are many worse places to be than on a beach in North Carolina."

When he has a rare moment to himself, James likes to take out his notebook. This English major has been crafting short stories, plays, and scripts since high school. "I like to write," he said to *16* magazine. "I write prose and a couple of short plays — mostly for myself to practice. I finished a screenplay but it's in no condition to be shot because I don't know everything about the technical side of film. But it's actually a lot of fun to try and write something."

He's also been practicing a new hobby. "I'm teaching myself how to play the guitar," he revealed to E! online. He's never at a loss for something to do when not in front of the camera. "I'll read, write, or in the case of this show, catch up on my sleep. I'll also join in whatever pickup games are going on."

Despite the success of *Dawson's Creek*, performing live onstage in the theater remains one of James's passions. In fact, he spent his winter hiatus from the first season searching out short-term work on the New York stage. Sounding very Dawson-like, he offered some valuable tips for other would-be young thespians to E! online. "Acting is the most unstable, unreliable, heart-wrenching career to choose," he said. "If you can do anything else and still find fulfillment, do it. Should you find yourself cursed with the undying passion to act, then the most important thing is to keep your eyes and ears open. Ask questions. Learn from everyone you can. The minute you stop learning, it's time to quit."

For now, James is very proud to be a part of the success of *Dawson's Creek*. "I can be a bit of a nut, but I am quite serious about this," he said in the *Orange County Register*. "Our message is, 'Give your kids credit because they're a lot smarter than you think they are.'" James is certainly one excellent example of that!

3

Say Hi to Katie

Still waters run deep, and that's certainly true of the character Joey Potter on *Dawson's Creek*. As played by nineteen-year-old Katie Holmes, Joey flashes her dark brown eyes to give us a glimpse into her soul. What she says is not always what she means, but we get it — even if her best buddy Dawson is too blind to truly see. Whether she's puzzling over her most recent change of heart about Dawson, figuring out whether she likes or hates Jen, or trying to come to terms with the devastating death of her mom, it's hard not to feel sympathy and love for such a complex but true-to-life girl.

One of Joey's most startling characteristics is how extremely blunt she can be. "My character says things people think but would never say out loud," Katie told *Teen People*. But that's one of the reasons she's so fun to watch on *Dawson's Creek* — you never know what she'll say next! It was the terrific dialogue that made her sure she wanted to play Joey. "When I read the script, I loved it. I can relate to it so much. [Writer Kevin Williamson] captures the voice of teenagers so well," she noted in *USA Today*.

For Joey, being sarcastic is a way to avoid revealing what she's really feeling. Her biggest fear is exposing her vulnerable heart. Her sharp tongue and quick put-downs are her best defense against a hostile world. As Katie explained to *Seventeen* magazine, "Joey *has* to come back with her wit. It's the only way she knows how to deal with her tough circumstances."

Hard-Knock Life

Joey's home life is the least stable of the four main characters on *Dawson's Creek*. She lives with her older sister — a new mother complete with a live-in boyfriend. Her family doesn't have much money. She watched her mom lose her battle with cancer less than two years ago, and her dad is out of the picture, too — he's serving jail time on drug charges. Clearly, Joey is a girl with lots of angst.

"She's sort of got a hard row to hoe," Kevin Williamson told a roomful of TV reporters at a *Dawson's Creek* press conference. "She's had to deal with a lot early on — particularly the death of her mother. She'll explore it. I don't think it's hit her yet."

Kevin admits that while a lot of Joey's characteristics are based on his childhood best friend, Fanny, the tragedies Joey suffers in her life are actually more a part of Kevin's own biography. "A lot of Joey's background is fictitious; some is based on my family," he said at the press conference. "The hard times Joey has experienced were adapted from the hard times my family had while I was growing up."

Joey's friendship with Dawson is the one reliable relationship in her life. As his best friend from earliest childhood, she is welcomed into his family, so much so that his parents don't care if she sleeps over whenever she wants. "My character has a lot of emotional baggage and Dawson is the only stable thing she has," said Katie to *16*.

Added writer Kevin, "It's just a very close relationship — Mom, Dad, Joey, Dawson. They've sort of taken her under their wing. She's part of the family." The fact that Joey ignores the front door and climbs through Dawson's window "just sort of defines their relationship," opined Katie at a Los Angeles press conference. "They're so comfortable. She just climbs up the ladder. She's been doing that her whole life."

Best friend or not, Joey has a tendency to get a little frustrated with Dawson. Living inside his head, he's sometimes insensitive to her feelings. She also thinks he's clueless about the really important things in life. "Joey sort of sees [Dawson] as this person who has this perfect, wonderful life. I mean, he's worried about his movie, when in Joey's opinion, he should be down on his knees thanking God he has the basics in life — like a mother," explained Kevin.

But Dawson's refusal to see what's real isn't the only thing that provokes Joey. She's often dazed about their relationship. He's her best friend, but then again, she wonders if they could be something more. Although she won't admit it, the attraction between Jen and Dawson makes Joey green with envy. "Only a few girls get to be prom queen and get all the guys. Those girls are like Jen," Katie told *Seventeen*. "Joey isn't the girl who gets all the guys. I wasn't like that, either, so I can relate."

But Joey isn't sure she actually wants Dawson as more than a friend. The only thing she knows for certain is she won't let anyone get in the way of their special relationship. "The new girl, Jen, arrives and kind of scares Joey a little because she's invading her territory," explained Katie to *16* magazine. At times, Joey almost lets her guard down around Jen, but then she gets scared and insecure again, fearing this new blond girl from the big city will steal the only stable person in her life.

Although Katie is more mature and experienced than Joey, it wasn't so long ago that she felt just as confused about life and, especially, guys. "It's nice to be older because you can look at the big picture, you can remember how you felt," she said in an online chat with Ultimate TV. "I relate to it so much — I was just there."

A Different Life

Katie and Joey share similar emotions in real life, but there are key differences. "She's shy at first, but when she gets to know someone she's not shy," Katie said of her character. "[Joey] tells it like it is and doesn't hold back. I kind of hold things in. She's more of a tomboy, rough around the edges. I'm a little more laid-back. Joey's full of emotions. I'm like her in that we both say what we feel, but Joey goes a little further. I wouldn't say a lot of the things she says."

Katie's family life is not at all like Joey's, which is probably a good thing. Katie was born in Toledo, Ohio, on December 18, 1978. She's the youngest of five very close siblings who were raised quite conservatively. "I come from a small city, and I was very, very sheltered," she said at a *Dawson's Creek* press conference. "At fifteen, I was, I think, concerned with just my friends still liking me and trying out for high school plays. My family is a large part of my life."

In fact, Katie grew up idolizing her older brother and three sisters. She wanted to do everything they were doing. She soon discovered, however, that not every kid has the same talents, even in the same family. "I come from a family of athletes who all play basketball," she revealed to *Teen Machine* magazine. "But athletic ability did not enter my body."

Katie says that although she was extremely frustrated with her lack of athletic ability, it really was a blessing in disguise because it led her to discover her other talents. "When I was little, I attempted to play basketball and softball, *attempted* being the key word here. The truth is, I was horrible at sports!" she confessed. "I realized that it wasn't my thing, but I had to do *something*. So I tried going out for parts in the musicals at my school." She got most of the parts she auditioned for.

In addition to acting and singing in school musicals, Katie filled her after-school hours with classes in jazz and ballet dancing. She also struggled through piano lessons for seven years. "I am still not very good at that," she admitted.

If Katie is slightly shy about her musical ability, she's not at all bashful about acting. "I did a lot of high school plays," she recalled for *Tiger Beat*. "I took a few classes in Toledo in a local modeling school, but I haven't really had any professional training or anything like that. I just kind of watch a lot of movies and use my imagination, I guess."

In the summer of her junior year, Katie explored the opportunities available to her beyond Toledo's city limits. "I went to an international modeling and talent convention in New York City," she explained. "I met my manager there." With professional representation Katie bagged her first movie — *The Ice Storm.*

A Dream Come True

Based on a book of the same name, *The Ice Storm* tells the story of a suburban Connecticut family weathering the changing morality of the 1970s. The film stars adult actors Sigourney Weaver, Joan Allen, and Kevin Kline, as well as teenage movie veterans Christina Ricci, Elijah Wood, and Tobey Maguire. Although the role of New York rich girl Libbets Casey wasn't the largest in the ensemble, Katie was thrilled just to be in such great company. "Working with talented people is wonderful," Katie enthusiastically told Ultimate TV. "I was fortunate enough to work with Tobey Maguire. It was great. He's a very talented actor . . . and a great friend." Katie's character, Libbets, is a wealthy prep school girl who catches the eye of Paul Hood, Tobey's character. "I play the love interest," said Katie online. "We have this little party . . . and Tobey hits on me."

The Ice Storm, which came out in 1997, won several prestigious awards, including Best Screenplay of the year at the famous Cannes Film Festival. Although Christina Ricci and most of the adult cast attended the film festival's screening of *The Ice Storm* in France, sensible Katie stayed behind in Toledo to finish up her senior year's final exams. She graduated from her all-girls high school with a 3.8 grade point average and was accepted to New York's Columbia University. Joey would be majorly envious.

Dawson's Waiting!

In show biz lingo, a pilot is the first, or sample, episode of a proposed new TV show. February in Los Angeles is pilot season — the time when those shows are cast. It's practically an annual rite of passage for actors looking to fill roles in those TV series and in films. Although she had luck the previous year landing *The Ice Storm*, Katie declined to travel out to Los Angeles during her all-important senior year of high school. She was afraid she would miss too much in her classes. "I wanted to be an actress, but I'm from Ohio," she told *Seventeen*. "I told myself, get a grip." Rather than fly all the way to California for meetings she thought might amount to nothing, Katie mailed off a videotape of her *Dawson's Creek* audition to the show's producers. Then she forgot about it.

But Charles Rosin and Paul Stupin, both of whom had previously worked on *Beverly Hills, 90210*, couldn't forget Katie. The *Dawson's Creek* producers liked her take on Joey so much that they invited her out to California for the second round of auditions. Although it was flattering, the invitation left Katie with an awful dilemma. She had been rehearsing for weeks to play Lola in her high school's production of *Damn Yankees*, and going to California would mean missing opening night. She didn't want to let down her school cast mates, and she really didn't want to miss out on something she'd worked so very hard for.

In fact, school and school activities have always been a priority to Katie. She excelled at most of her subjects and tolerated the ones she didn't love. She had her own clique of friends — mostly girls who were good students like herself and who were interested in movies, plays, and sports. "A good friend of mine is a basketball player and so I go to all of her games," she told *Tiger Beat*.

So, even if going to California meant a chance at a TV series, Katie wasn't about to just drop her commitment to her school play. In a bold move, she called the office of *Dawson's Creek* producer Paul Stupin and asked if her audition could be postponed. The producers actually agreed to wait for her, and Katie flew to California the day after *Damn Yankees'* final performance. She then wowed the producers and snagged the plum role of Joey!

On the Set

Moving to North Carolina was the biggest adjustment for Katie, who had never been away from home before. She's extremely close to her family and spends many, many hours on the phone with them back in Ohio. They, in turn, have been thrilled for Katie and one hundred percent behind her sudden career. "My brother is a lawyer. My sister is a physical therapist. They all have normal jobs, so this is all very new and exciting," she told *Tiger Beat*. "They are all very supportive."

41

She confesses that in the whirlwind of attention she's received from *Dawson's Creek*, her family has been instrumental in keeping her ego in check. They would never let the baby of the clan suddenly think she was hot stuff. Katie confesses, "If I did that my family would knock me over the side of my head, like, 'Who do you think you are?'"

In Wilmington, Katie lives in an apartment above a video store just a few blocks from the digs shared by Josh and James. Although she and Michelle have become really good friends, Katie nixed the idea of rooming together, feeling she was best suited for living alone. "I'm not the easiest person to live with," she confessed to *Seventeen*. "I'm kind of a slob. So for me to consider a roommate, it would have to be one of my sisters or something." Even though they don't live together, Katie and Michelle have had many girls' "bonding" nights, complete with take-out pizza and videos of '80s teen comedies like *Pretty in Pink* and *The Breakfast Club*. They like to bake cookies, take trips to the beach to soak up the sun, and visit larger cities within driving distance for shopping — one of Katie's favorite hobbies.

When it comes to style, Katie's not into designer duds. Her preferred look is casual and slightly preppy. It's no wonder she looked so comfortable modeling J. Crew clothes with the rest of the gang in the winter 1998 catalogue! "My style is very conservative," she confessed to *16*. "But I like bell bottoms and that Urban Outfitters-type clothing for weekends. I wear a lot of browns and blacks — I like those colors."

Another of Katie's favorite pastimes is running. No, she hasn't suddenly become the superjock she wanted to be as a kid, but she's found that running solo, at her own pace while listening to her favorite music, is a good way to ease the tension of a busy life. "Running really helps clear my head and makes me feel good, especially when I'm stressed. Lately, I've been doing it several times a week. Nothing long-distance or anything, just like three or four miles each time," she told *Jump*. "It's pretty cool."

Beyond the Creek

Education has always been very important to Katie. If she hadn't won the role of Joey, she'd absolutely be in college right now. "I've

43

been accepted to Columbia," she explained to *USA Today,* "and I've deferred for this year. Eventually, I'll go back. I want to major in English, but that'll probably change next month!"

The success Katie is experiencing in Hollywood right now means she might have to wait longer than she expects! In fact, while the entire cast is experiencing instant fame, Katie's being hailed as the *Dawson's Creek* break-out star. Since the show's debut, she's been on the covers of several teen magazines *and* booked three movies.

How does Katie feel about becoming a star overnight? "It was a dream," she said in an online interview. "Going from a high school musical to this. Getting to meet all these people, forming all these friendships, and all this buzz . . . It's crazy!"

Naturally, all this work leaves little time for dating, but Katie admits she's definitely not immune to the charms of a really cute guy. "I like a great sense of humor, a good personality, and someone with a little spunkiness," she told *Tiger Beat.* "Tall, dark, and handsome." It also helps if a prospective boyfriend has a romantic side. "I like the beach," she said. "I think the beach is romantic. Also, going out to dinner and maybe flowers."

And, if you've been wondering . . . no, Katie isn't interested in dating any of her costars. Joey may have a thing for Dawson, but Katie and James are just pals. "There's nothing romantic about it," she's insisted. "We have more of a brother–sister kind of relationship. We pull pranks on each other, that kind of stuff, but I've never thought of him in any other way. We all try to stay professional."

Although Katie is too busy for a steady relationship with a guy right now, she doesn't want to rule it out in the future. Where does she expect to be in ten years? "Married, with one-point-five children," she said with a laugh in an Ultimate TV online chat. "I hope I'm at a nice place in my career. I hope I'm starting college or have already gone. I hope I'm in love!"

She'd also like to stretch her wings and do more movies. Katie's wish list of folks with whom she aspires to work extends from Oliver Stone to Woody Allen. "I want to do things that are interesting and help me grow as an actor. [I want to] do projects that make me happy."

Because, she says, being happy is what life is all about. "Success," she explained to *Seventeen* magazine, "is about getting an education and being happy. I'm taking each day as it comes. I'm just having fun."

4

It's Josh

Pacey Witter is the best friend a guy could have. Funny, good-natured, and loyal, he's one of a kind. It's too bad none of the girls at Capeside High School, or even many of the guys, recognize the strong points of the self-acknowledged class clown. To most, Pacey is just a joke. "Pacey's basically an outsider at school who also feels disconnected from his family. He's always been told he's a screw-up and isn't going to succeed, so he feels he can do anything he likes and has nothing to lose," explained actor Joshua Jackson in an interview with *Teen Machine*. "He's in his own world, doing his own thing, which, unfortunately, seems to offend a lot of people."

Sadly, the people who disapprove of Pacey the most are his father and his older brother, Doug. "His father is the sheriff of Capeside and his brother is a deputy," said Josh. "Pacey is the youngest, oddball child in an authoritative family. The only way he can deal is to be as big a screw-up as possible."

Series creator Kevin Williamson adds, "He's just this character who puts himself out there. More times than not, he gets stepped on, because that's who Pacey is."

Laughter Through Tears

For actor Joshua Jackson — Josh, as his friends call him — becoming Pacey was not difficult. "I'm a lot like Pacey. Well, that's kind of my personality—a goofball!" he told *Teen Machine* with a laugh. As a teenager, he also encountered similar feelings of worthlessness and not belonging. "Four years ago, I had similar issues to what Pacey is dealing with," he said. "We both grew up in a community-based atmosphere. He grew up in a much smaller town, which has its own limitations and benefits, but I grew up in a community where I knew everybody in the neighborhood, went to school with all the same kids, and spent a decade of my life with the same people."

Both Josh's and Pacey's senses of humor run to the offbeat. "I enjoy laughing, having a good time, and often get myself in trouble for it. But neither of us is mischievous for mischief's sake." Said simply by roommate and costar James to *Seventeen* magazine, "Josh is bizarre." Of course, he said it with a smile.

He's also modest. "I wish I could sell you on the fact that I'm a great actor, but it's just not the truth. I wish that I was a really dour man who could put on a great character, but I was typecast," he told *Tiger Beat*. "It's fun being a little bit goofy and I'm like that in real life anyway." He added to E!, "I *was* that guy at fifteen, and I *am* that guy now. I haven't been acting for the last six months; I've just been showing up and being myself. We're exactly the same."

Although modest Josh might downplay the challenge of playing Pacey, he's done a great job of showing the heart behind the comic quips. No matter how many silly things Pacey says, Josh feels the character's actions speak louder than words. In fact, they're often worthy of respect. "He has some wonderful redeeming qualities that I wish I could live by all the time in my life," said Josh during an interview with *Tiger Beat*. He pointed to the admirable way Pacey stood up for his teacher Tamara Jacobs when the school board began the investigation of their rumored romantic relationship. "That's one of the defining moments of his life, when he steps up and takes the heat — and saves her reputation, even at the cost of his own. It's like, do you shrink away or do you step up and take the pain and grin and bear it like a man? It's a great thing to do. I really like that," Josh added.

For Josh, the real challenge of playing Pacey is balancing the comic with the caring. "A lot of times the sidekick character will just be the sidekick character. Like, hey, there's crazy Pacey! But on the other side, I think I've got some, I hope, really heartwarming and touching stuff," he said in an interview. "So, hopefully, you get to see the flip side of the coin."

Sitting Duck

Joshua Jackson was born on June 11, 1978, in Vancouver, Canada. He spent the first eight years of his life in California before moving back to Canada with his family. Naturally outgoing and energetic, he always loved to be the center of attention. He bugged his mom, Fiona, a casting director, to let him try auditioning for movies and TV after watching other kids on television. Knowing how heartbreaking the entertainment industry can be, Fiona brought her persistent nine-year-old son on an audition for a commercial promoting tourism in Vancouver and British Columbia in hopes that *not* being picked for the job would discourage his interest in acting. Oops! Much to his mom's chagrin, Josh got the part!

From that time on, Fiona promised to help him pursue acting jobs. As a kid, Josh worked as an extra on the TV series *MacGyver*, which filmed in Vancouver. He won his first role in a movie, *Crooked Hearts*, in 1991. "I was in the first ten minutes or so. I played the young Peter Berg [of *Chicago Hope*]," he said in an interview. "It also had Vincent D'Onofrio, Noah Wyle, Juliette Lewis, and a bunch of others. Wyle and Berg were very cool and took us out all the time."

Although he thinks of himself as a Canadian all the way, Josh and his family split their time between Vancouver and California. That's why, while Josh was growing up, he was able to both sing with the San Francisco Boys' Chorus *and* play ice hockey with his buds in Canada. His aptitude at the latter really came in handy during his auditions for 1992's *The Mighty Ducks.*

Remember the episode of *Dawson's Creek* where the entire gang got Saturday detention — and Pacey mentioned that *The Mighty Ducks* movies were "classics"? That was an in-joke — since Josh Jackson starred in all three.

Josh played the Ducks' straitlaced hockey prodigy, Charlie Conway, in the original and both sequels to the Disney hit film. Until *Dawson's Creek,* the *Ducks* movies were his biggest claim to fame. Josh is still quite proud of those movies. "To adult America, *The Mighty Ducks* is a blip on the screen," he said to *USA Today.* "But to kids, it's a big deal. It's very much a part of how kids grow up."

Josh admits that working on *The Mighty Ducks* was probably the most fun he will ever have on a film set. "It was like a case study for young children," he said during an online interview about reteaming with his costars for the sequels. "You'd relearn these people every two years. We had a lot of fun, too, [because] we were getting paid to play hockey."

Until *Dawson's Creek* splashed his face on billboards all over the country, Josh could go about his life as a regular teenager without being recognized as an actor very often. When he *was* recognized, it was for his *Ducks* role. "Sometimes people would come up and ask about *Mighty Ducks* — usually little kids and it's kind of cute. They'll ask how the team is doing and I'll tell them all the guys are doing great."

Of course, there are times when *Ducks* mania gets to be a little bit much. "There've been a couple of incidents," he reported. "Once I was in Canada for American Thanksgiving. My sister goes to school on Vancouver Island, and you have to take a ferry. This girl came up to me and said, 'You're Charlie from *Mighty Ducks*.' It was sweet and flattering, but then she proceeded to get the other three busloads of kids, and I spent the next hour answering questions about *The Mighty Ducks*!"

Then again, sometimes the perks of having been a Duck are pretty nice. "Actually, I got my license plate free at the DMV because the lady had seen *Mighty Ducks*," he said in an online chat. "I took out my wallet, and she said, 'Honey, your money's no good here.'"

Josh credits *Mighty Ducks* star Emilio Estevez for teaching him how to behave like a professional on a film set. "Emilio was a very big influence. Watching him work was great. He's a world-class guy — he shows up on time, knows his lines, he's good to the crew, amiable — basically he's what all actors should be instead of having an attitude or being unpleasant. I learned the fine points of etiquette from him."

Though *The Mighty Ducks* movies will always remain a happy memory for Josh, he doubts the team will be reuniting anytime soon for a new feature. "Every once in a while, there's a rumor that a fourth installment is coming, but I have the feeling that if they did, they'd bring in younger kids — our cute factor is running out," he told *E!* "But I'd love to pass the torch because I had a great time doing it."

Perfectly Pacey

With the help of his mom, Joshua did a great job balancing his acting assignments with an almost typical high school career. (In addition to *The Mighty Ducks* films, he appeared in the movies *Digger*, *Andre*, and *Magic in the Water*.) Like his *Dawson's Creek* character, he liked to goof around in school. "I tended to be pretty average," he admitted about his grades to *Bop* magazine. His favorite subjects, he joked, were recess and lunch. "If I did more work, I probably would have done a little better."

During his senior year, Josh filmed the Showtime cable movies *Robin of Locksley* (where he played the bad guy opposite Devon Sawa) and *Ronnie and Julie*, a '90s update of *Romeo and Juliet*. He took some time off to travel after graduation before landing back in Los Angeles in 1997.

A little known fact is that Josh auditioned for both the roles of Pacey *and* Dawson on *Dawson's Creek*. "I just happened to be in L.A. and went in and read for Pacey. The next day, they had me read Dawson. Then they said never mind," he recalled with a laugh. "Then they called again for me to read for Pacey. It took about five days. On my way walking out, they said, 'Hey, by the way, we'll see you in North Carolina.'"

Does Josh think he could have played Dawson instead of Pacey? "Yes, I could have," he said during an online chat. "But I wouldn't have brought the same things to the part that [James] does. So the short answer is no, and the long answer is yes. I could have, but you wouldn't be enjoying the show as much."

Josh is perfectly happy playing Pacey. Like many fans of *Dawson's Creek*, he wondered where Kevin dreamed up his character's unusual name. "I asked about it when I auditioned. It's actually the name of one of Kevin Williamson's best friends growing up." And like Kevin and the real Pacey, Josh's fictional character and his best friend, Dawson, have a very special relationship. "I think he clings so hard to Dawson because he's the only person Pacey can really hang out with and be who he wants to be."

Doggone It!

On the set in Wilmington, Josh and costar James share their apartment with Josh's lovable but enormous dog, a Rhodesian Ridgeback and black Labrador mix appropriately named Shumba, which means "lion" in Swahili. Although Shumba is likely to follow Josh everywhere he goes, Josh still claims that he and his fellow castmates don't really stand out in Wilmington. "We just sort of blend in as teenagers," he explained in a *Tiger Beat* interview.

"I like it there because it's so small and it's a film community," Josh said. "It's a place where the cast can go about our lives almost anonymously. The town is actually the third-largest production base in North America, so no one's really impressed with having the *Dawson's Creek* cast there."

Living, working, and playing together, Josh, James, Michelle, and Katie have all gotten to know one another very, very well, even if they're beyond their "honeymoon period." "We did the pilot and got along famously in the beginning," Josh revealed to a reporter from *TV Hits*. "It was kind of funny because when we first got down there we sort of went everywhere together. We didn't know anybody else, so we were inseparable. Now, we have our ups and downs but, generally speaking, we're a pretty harmonious group. The cast is really one big family. We're really tight. It's like having brothers and sisters. There are fights and squabbles, ups and downs, but we get along really well."

But when practical jokes happen on the set, the cast and crew tend to look suspiciously in Josh's direction. Can you blame them? "I'm a practical joker. I always play jokes on the grips and electrical guys," he confessed to E! One day, the crew decided to get even. "In *The Breakfast Club* episode, we run through the hall, and I'm supposed to come crashing through a door, but the grips had locked the door on me, and we did, like, a Three Stooges thing with all of us like dominoes hitting the door. After I woke up from my concussion, [he joked] I thought it was really funny."

Josh counts himself very lucky to be among the cast of *Dawson's Creek*. "The hours are long, you work pretty hard, and it can get pretty tough. It's very tiring because we don't have a lot of time — in movies there's more time," he said to *Tiger Beat*. "Still, I'm a nineteen-year-old kid getting paid to be on a TV show, so I can't complain. It's working out quite nicely."

Oh, Canada!

Dawson's Creek has made Josh a better-known actor. In fact, he joked to E!, "If I see my face on a poster one more time, I'm probably going to be ill." No matter how well-known he's become, Josh still claims to be a Hollywood outsider. "If Hollywood is a state of mind, then I'm an ignorant man," he said. "Home for me is Vancouver, Canada." In fact, while Katie and Michelle flew off to start working on new movie projects when the *Dawson's Creek* production wrapped the first season in December 1997, Josh bagged work and instead went home to Vancouver to visit his mom and younger sister.

The bond Josh shares with the ladies in his family is another trait he has in common with his *Dawson's Creek* character. "Pacey is closer to his mother and sisters, but his sisters are off at school. Because of this family dynamic, Pacey is much more comfortable with women," he has explained. "I was raised among females; it was just me, my mom, and my sister, and I'm more comfortable being around women because of that, too." Josh is still extremely close to his mom, Fiona, and his younger sister, Aisleegh. He makes time to do something fun with them whenever he's home. "Since I'm away from home a lot, I like to catch up with my mom and little sister and just do fun things with my friends, like pickup hockey games and stuff like that," he told *Tiger Beat*. "Just basically hang out with my family and friends in Vancouver. Just typical stuff for a nineteen-year-old."

Josh jokes about his "gainful unemployment," while on break — as opposed to how his female costars are spending *their* off time.

"I'm back home relaxing," he said during a winter break chat with E! online. "But Katie's doing, like thirty-five movies, and Michelle is in [the movie] *Halloween H2O*. The girls' careers are taking off; we're the shlubs."

Makin' Movies

But don't let him fool you, Josh isn't a complete "shlub"! While filming *Dawson's Creek,* he jumped at the chance to play a small role — as a college film student in Kevin Williamson's *Scream 2*. "That was awesome," he said to *Tiger Beat*. "I mean, here I was working in North Carolina on *Dawson's Creek*. Kevin comes up to me and says, 'Josh, I don't know if you want to do this, but I think I have this fun thing for you to do, but it's all the way in L.A. Would you like to do a cameo in *Scream 2*?' I'm like, '*Scream 2*? Oh, that little thing you have going on? Of course, I would!' So, I got flown out there and they put me up at the nicest hotel. I had a driver and got to be real cool. I even got to meet Neve Campbell!"

Although Josh isn't normally starstruck,

he had a personal reason for wanting to meet the pretty star of *Party of Five*. "Ever since I was a little kid, I went through this punk rock phase and my dream woman was, like, this girl in combat boots with short dark hair," he confided during an interview. "And that's Neve! She shows up and she's wearing the combat boots, the dark hair, and the spiked collar and I'm like, I love you!"

Before his *Scream 2* cameo, and months prior to *Dawson's Creek*, Josh acted in the movie *Apt Pupil*. In it, Brad Renfro stars as a teenager who suspects that his neighbor is a war criminal. Josh plays Brad's best friend. Based on a short story by Stephen King, the movie also stars veteran actor Ian McKellen as the man under suspicion. Josh told E!, "The script is close to the original story, but since that was a short story, this is an expanded version. It's very disturbing — just really dark, dark stuff." Josh admits that watching Ian McKellen work was a slightly creepy experience. "I didn't get to work on camera with him too much," said Josh in an online interview with Ultimate TV. "He's always in character on set, which is kind of disturbing because he plays a war criminal. It was wild seeing him work [like that]."

Just for Fun

When Josh isn't working, he likes to play sports. His time as a Mighty Duck served him well because he's still a demon on ice. This six-foot-tall teenager played high school football and still enjoys a chance to throw around the pigskin with his costars. Shumba, his dog, much prefers playing catch with a Frisbee. In fact, Shumba even joined Josh and the rest of the *Dawson's Creek* cast in the pages of J. Crew's winter 1998 catalogue.

Both Josh and his pooch enjoy living part of the year in North Carolina. "Wilmington in the summer is like a resort. After you wrap, you put on the swim trunks and go jump into the ocean," said Josh to E! "In the winter, it's a little different. If I wasn't working, I don't know what I'd do. I can't go to clubs because I'm not old enough. It's a beautiful town, but I'm glad to be working while I'm there."

Although his crazy *Dawson's Creek* schedule doesn't allow much time to watch TV, Josh admits that he likes to keep up with *The X-Files*. Some of his other favorites include rap music and acid jazz, the movies *Good Will Hunting* and *Pulp Fiction*, worn old sneakers, traveling to Ireland, and cute girls who laugh at his jokes. Although he's still waiting for

Neve Campbell to come around and date him — !! — Josh doesn't go out with actresses. "If I only dated actresses, I'd be a very lonely man," he quipped. "My first love was not an actress: five-six, curly brown hair, cute as a button — an absolute sweetheart."

Josh enjoys acting a lot, but he's had enough experience in the business to know that he may not be able to do it forever. "I intend to go back to school," he told a reporter. "The show will provide me with a nice nest egg so I'll be able to go to college and study for what I want to do with the rest of my life. If I could stay in the business, who knows? I have experience and it's rewarding, but acting is really a fleeting job, so I'll have to be prepared." Although Josh briefly flirted with the idea of becoming an architect or an archaeologist, right now he's most interested in studying English and philosophy. No matter what he decides to do, it's clear that Josh will always face the future with a laugh and a smile!

5

Hanging With Michelle

It's always tough to be the new kid in town. There's pressure to leave the past behind and start all over again. With a swirl of curiosity following your every move, you try to do everything possible to fit in. That's the story of Capeside's newest arrival, New York City girl Jennifer Lindley — or Jen to her new friends — whose greatest wish is to forget the incidents of her recent past and start living a simpler teenage life on *Dawson's Creek*.

Jen's appearance in Capeside the day before school starts is immediately noticed by Dawson and Pacey. Dawson reacts like he's been hit by Cupid's arrow, while Pacey, well . . .

he can't help but make some rude joking remarks. Joey, who is also standing on the dock
when Jen hits town, can't help but feel a little
territorial. After all, she's known Dawson and
Pacey forever and they've never been lovesick
over her, ever!

Joey's also suspicious of the new girl's
story. Jen claims to have come to help her
grandmother tend to her grandfather through
his recent illness. But Joey knows that Jen's
grandmother is a former nurse and a strict,
old-fashioned busybody with all the disci-
pline of a marine drill sergeant. She hardly
seems to need the help! Joey decides something else is definitely going on. But Dawson,
who's off in puppy-love dreams of Jen, just
doesn't seem to get it.

Secrets and Lies

For Jen, moving to Capeside is a chance to
catch her breath and figure out who she
really is. Her life in New York had been spin-
ning wildly out of control. Her party-girl
ways had alarmed her parents, who decided
to send her to live with Grams, as Jen calls
her grandmother, in hopes the change would
help her remember what's really important
in life. "I think a part of Jen is really looking

to regain her innocence and lead the quintessential teenage life," said Michelle to reporters at a *Dawson's Creek* press conference. "She wants to fit in with these more carefree kids. But there's another part of her that still longs for the city lights. She made some mistakes and got sent to Capeside by her parents in hopes that she'd begin to realize she should slow down and change her ways."

Jen, however, needs more than good intentions to really change her own heart. One of her most important guides in her journey to a new life is her strict, extremely religious grandmother. Although the affection between Grams and Jen is genuine, Jen often ignores her grandmother's words, dismissing them as hopelessly ancient. However, as Jen begins to spend more time with her grandmother, she learns that she isn't as Jurassic as she first believed. "There's a wonderful dynamic where Jen says, 'Grams, open your mind,' and Jen ultimately realizes it's *her* mind that's not opening," revealed *Dawson's Creek* writer Kevin Williamson to New York's *Newsday*.

For Michelle, playing Jen has been a wonderful, surprise-filled challenge. "She really began to unfold from being someone who is relatively stable and happy-go-lucky, to some-

Dorothy Low/Shooting Star

JAMES VAN DER BEEK plays Dawson Leery.

Was James fated to play the title role in *Dawson's Creek*? After all, his last name is Dutch for "by the brook."

BEFORE HE WAS DAWSON

New Line Cinema/Shooting Star

In 1996's *Angus,* James played a high school bully. He based his character on real life—only *he* was the one bullied!

A portrait from James' first photo shoot for a teen magazine—it was 1996.

JOSH JACKSON plays Pacey Witter.

BEFORE HE WAS PACEY

Meila Penn, Everett Collection

Josh was best known as Charlie from *The Mighty Ducks* movies—he costarred with Vincent LaRusso in this scene from the third installment.

Josh and Adam Hann-Byrd were buddies in *Digger*—a little-seen flick.

Photofest

Did you know that Josh also auditioned to
play Dawson? No joke!

KATIE HOLMES plays Joey Potter.

So are there any behind-the-scenes romances? James and Katie say—no way!

Katie's slated to appear in three new movies—is she the breakout star of *Dawson's Creek*, or what?

Pacha/Corbis

The gang dresses up mostly never—
except for formal interview sessions! But
they're always kidding around, especially
Pacey...that is, Josh.

MICHELLE WILLIAMS plays Jen Lindley.

BEFORE SHE WAS JEN

Michelle costarred in the family movie *Lassie* with Tommy Guiry—and, Lassie!

Jen and Dawson hung out for a while—but no romance developed between Michelle and James. They're just pals.

Paramount/Shooting Star

Walter McBribe/Retna

Though she neither rocks, nor claims jock bragging rights, Michelle gamely suited up for the charity-driven MTV Rock 'N' Jock Celebrity Softball Game.

Though James is psyched to be Dawson,
he claims his real love is the stage.

Josh is never lonely on the *Dawson's Creek* location—his dog Shumba lives with him.

Katie's stylin' in a white pants suit and strappy sandals.

Michelle goes for geometic-pattern tube dresses and ankle-strap platforms.

It's the end
of something simple.

And the beginning
of everything else.

DAWSON'S CREEK

KEVIN
WILLIAMSON

JAMES   MICHELLE JOSHUA KATIE
VAN DER BEEK WILLIAMS JACKSON HOLMES

TUESDAYS ON THE WB

The *Dawson's Creek* poster wouldn't be hanging in Dawson's room, but can be found on the walls of fans all over America.

one who is wrestling with some demons," she told the *Chicago Tribune*. "She grew up quickly," she added. "She's an old soul, having done too much too soon." Michelle relates to her character so much so that "playing Jen is like slipping on a second skin," she told *YM* magazine. "I certainly have a lot to draw upon; everybody's got a past."

Life on the Fast Track

Michelle is sure the parallels in her and Jen's lives are part of the reason she was chosen to star on *Dawson's Creek*. "I think there are a lot of similarities between the character of Jen and me," she told *Teen Machine*. "She went out on her own at an early age and grew up in a big city by herself, like me, so it's not too hard to relate to that." In fact, she noted, every *Dawson's Creek* cast member is playing someone very similar to him or herself. "That's why we were cast, because it's so easy for us to get into these characters. It's really not too much of a departure," she told *TV Hits*.

Although Michelle is the youngest cast member of the series, she's actually the one who's had the most life experience. She was living on her own in Los Angeles before being cast as the girl with a secret history. When she celebrated her seventeenth birthday while shooting the show, she had already been in the entertainment business for a full decade!

Michelle was born in the small rural town of Kalispell, Montana. "It was wide open, beautiful — and cold," she told *YM*. "One winter, the temperature was lower than thirty below zero every day for over a month. That was it, my parents packed us up, and we all moved to San Diego [California]."

Michelle spent the rest of her childhood years in southern California where, at age eight, she discovered her passion for acting totally by accident. "My parents took me to a play, and I was mesmerized," she revealed. "I told them I wanted to perform on stage like that. I really felt I could do it."

She began taking acting classes and performing in community theater. She was always ambitious. Starting at the age of ten, Michelle made the three-hour drive to Los Angeles frequently with her parents so she could participate in commercial and TV auditions. This young actress admits that there was no possible career choice for her but acting. "No, nothing," she told *Teen*. "It's eat, sleep, act." At age twelve, she won her first TV appearance. Her credits include guest spots on hit TV shows like *Home Improvement* and *Step by Step*.

High School Horror!

Michelle spent a year at a public high school in San Diego, where she always felt like an outsider. "I did my freshman year at a normal high school," she told *Teen Machine*. "That year was crammed with all these kinds of terrible teenage experiences. So there was definitely some real-life experience to draw upon."

Michelle, a serious teenager who did well in her studies, had a really difficult time fitting in—which helped her to completely relate to Jen's dilemma on *Dawson's Creek*. "I remember feeling so different myself from all the other kids," she said in *YM*. "Jen is definitely from a different world than the kids at her new school. She's a New York girl who's been transplanted to a small, quiet New England town."

Michelle had an even more difficult time than Jen when it came to fitting in with the kids in her high school in San Diego. "If there were good times, I don't remember them," she said to *Teen*. "I had no friends, no one to talk to! I spent every lunch in the bathroom, hiding in a stall. I just hated the people, the atmosphere, and the catty fights between the girls. The girls just didn't understand that there was life beyond clothes, makeup, and boys."

Michelle confesses that she was a shy adolescent. Her budding acting career required her to miss a lot of days in the classroom, so she had a hard time making friends. "I was a total nerd!" she said to *YM*. "People really underestimate how tough high school can be for kids. There's pressure from all sides. You have to get good grades and look and act a certain way to fit in, and everyone thinks you need a boyfriend."

And other kids can be pretty mean. "There was this one girl who used to torture me. She stole my clothes out of my gym locker and hid them," she said in the same interview. "My personal favorite was the time she sent me a fake note from this very cute boy in my class. It read, 'Meet me by the back stairs at three.' Of course I felt like a big fool when I showed up and he wasn't there."

After her freshman year, Michelle left public high school and began earning her high school credits with a home tutor. An avid reader, she counts literary heavyweights Kurt

Vonnegut, Jr., Hermann Hesse, and Fyodor Dostoyevsky among her favorite authors. "I always enjoyed the work," she said of school in *Teen*. "Just not the social part of it." Working at her own pace with a tutor, Michelle received her diploma in just one more year, at the age of sixteen.

She absolutely has no regrets about choosing home schooling over a traditional classroom, but being on *Dawson's Creek* has given her a chance to experience some of the social things she missed. "We did a school dance episode and in real life I never went to any of those," she explained to *Teen Machine*. "So I got to live vicariously through my character. By having home school, there are a lot of things I didn't get to do — the dance, sitting behind a desk, hanging out at the lockers, and all that sort of stuff."

Happy in Hollywood

All during her school years, Michelle continued to act. In fact, her career was moving at a nice clip. Her silver-screen debut was in 1994 in an updated movie version of the classic TV show *Lassie*. A year later, she played the young alien Sil in the science fiction film *Species*. That movie gave her a brush with fame of a very different kind. "I don't think that I had any idea of the magnitude of this movie; I was a young teenager going to work and they put stuff on my face," said Michelle during an interview with Ultimate TV. "But then [the film] got this cult following. It was just a job for me. People would send me letters and ask me to come to their alien conventions. They took it as reality!"

In 1997, she appeared alongside veteran actresses Michelle Pfeiffer, Jennifer Jason Leigh, and Jessica Lange in the dramatic film *A Thousand Acres*. "It was very intimidating at first," she said in *YM*. "I was working with these famous actresses, and we were dealing with a very heavy subject. [But] they were helpful and sweet." She shared in an online interview with Ultimate TV, "I learned a lot; what I learned cannot be expressed in words. It was different things from the three of them; with Jessica it was about grace, Michelle is ethereal, [and] Jennifer is so complex."

Michelle's parents, Larry and Carla, were extremely supportive of her acting career, but commuting back and forth from Los Angeles to San Diego each day became pretty tiring. With the promise of more exciting projects to come, Michelle made the difficult decision to move out of her parents' home in San Diego and live in L.A. full-time. "I got an apartment in Burbank and my parents took turns living with me there," she explained to *YM*. That arrangement was difficult, because Michelle's younger sister, Paige, also needed her parents' time and attention. So at age sixteen, Michelle became legally emancipated — declared a legal adult by a judge — and was able to live on her own. "I've got a vicious independent streak," she explained in *Teen*. "I love being on my own. It's been a source of agony for my parents."

Happy as the arrangement made her, Michelle admits that moving away from home was the hardest decision she'd ever made. She tries to compensate for her absence with frequent phone calls home. "I miss my family," she told *YM*. "It's really hard to be away from my sister, Paige. She's fourteen and doing all these fun things, like going to homecoming. I have to give her advice over the phone instead of seeing her every day."

One of Those Days

Although Michelle didn't think she was interested in auditioning for a television series, especially one that would take her away from her beloved Los Angeles, she found herself hooked on *Dawson's Creek* from the moment she opened the pilot script. "I read this script, and I fell in love with it," she described. "It was more than just another script. I wanted it with all my heart, because the writing was so phenomenal. It was the honesty, the intelligence, and the integrity of the characters."

She was particularly impressed with how accurately *Dawson's Creek* depicted teenage life in the '90s. "The sense of reality is really very grounded, I mean, like the emotions, the fears, and the joys are exactly what I went through."

Michelle very clearly remembers the fear and joy she experienced the day she found out she won the role of Jen. Actually, getting *Dawson's Creek* was the *only* good thing that happened to her that day. "I simply had the worst day," she told *TV Hits*. "I'd been to the network and thought I'd completely screwed up the audition. Then I backed my car into a gas pump. I dropped my cell phone into this vat of some terrible liquid icky goop or something, and it, like, melted it. It was the worst day! Then, I get paged and the message was to call the network casting people back and I had no money for a pay phone! Absolutely nothing was going right! But they told me I'd gotten the part, so at least I could now afford to fix the big dent [in] my fender!"

That's not all Michelle could afford. Soon after completing the first season of *Dawson's Creek*, she flew back to Los Angeles and bought her very first house high up in the Hollywood Hills.

Life on the Creek

Maturity is not the only thing that Michelle shares with her *Dawson's Creek* character. Both she and Jen are city girls getting used to life in a small town. Michelle confessed that the move to Wilmington, North Carolina, was hard. "It's quite a change from Los Angeles," she said to *Tiger Beat*. "It's beautiful and a nice pace for a while, but at first it was a strange switch from the city and traffic. Having the experience of moving from a big city to a small town does make it easier to relate to Jen, however." She added in *Entertainment Weekly*, "The people are incredibly kind, but everything does move at a slower pace."

Clicking with her costars was a bonus. "We were really lucky," she said to *TV Hits*. "I mean, you're forced into a situation with people that you don't know, and you really don't get to choose who you're going to get to spend the next ten months with. So it's fabulous how well we've all gotten along, because we really had no choice. What if we hated each other?"

Dawson and Jen's attraction is a large story in the first season of *Dawson's Creek*. However, Michelle echoes Katie's assertion that behind the scenes, their relationships are not at all romantic. She would never dream of dating either of the *Dawson's Creek* boys! "James and Josh are like big brothers to me," she told *Teen Machine*. "They're constantly giving me noogies and all this stuff." She added in *TV Hits*, "It's like having two great older brothers who are there to look out for both Katie and [me]."

The cast's main group recreation is going out for meals together in downtown Wilmington. "They have the best restaurants here," she said in *Seventeen*. "We all have big appetites." But honestly, her favorite leisure time activity after a long day on the set is just going home, putting on some grungy old sweats, and reading a good book. "When you work with people five or six days a week, that's plenty," she told *Teen*. "I love all three of them to death, but I need a little time to myself!"

In Wilmington, Michelle has her own apartment just blocks away from the other cast members. She told *TV Hits* that she imagines their lives together were similar to what people experience in college. "You know, you work six days a week. You eat with them. All you do is basically get to go home and have three hours to yourself, so it really is like being in one big sorority. I mean it's such a small town we work in."

Although they don't live together, Michelle struck up a special friendship with her costar Katie. "There are only a few of us who are really young," she said in *YM*. "So Katie and I make a point of finding time to goof off and be kids. We also bake cookies and drink a lot of coffee. I'm pretty happy to have a buddy to do girl stuff with."

There are definitely times when the charm of this small southern city doesn't make up for the things she misses about her life in L.A., however. "The nightlife in North Carolina — it's just raging," she said sarcastically to *TV Hits*, sounding quite like Jen. "I miss breathing air that I can see. I really miss that smog; I need it for my lungs! I just don't know how to function without it," she joked. Michelle also misses having a variety of stores to shop in and the anonymity that living in a big city provides. "We've already started to feel [the attention] a little in North Carolina, because it's such a small town," she said in the same interview. "There's the Wal-Mart department store, the gas station, and a restaurant. We're mobbed by locals who had a cousin that was an extra on the show."

As soon as she returned to Los Angeles, Michelle treated herself to a purely L.A. kind of treat. "The first thing I did when I got back to L.A. was drive down Sunset Boulevard with the top off my car!" she told *Entertainment Weekly*.

Suddenly Famous

That Sunset Boulevard cruise was a bit of a shock for Michelle. It was the first time she saw her own face plastered on a giant billboard advertising the WB's hot new teen drama *Dawson's Creek*. "I was driving down Sunset Boulevard — just driving along singing to the radio — and I see one of those billboards and I screech to a stop," she told *Teen Machine*. The sudden exposure felt really strange, like it was happening to someone else. "It's kind of like I stepped out of my body and it just wasn't really me," she said. "It was this poster. I can't really look at it as myself. It's all just too weird."

Though she's gorgeous and talented, Michelle admitted to *TV Hits* that she's not really fond of seeing herself. "I can't — eeek! I've watched a few [episodes], but I get really hypercritical watching myself. I start wanting to change things and all that sort of stuff."

The fame game is something that Michelle is still trying to figure out. The first time she was recognized as a *Dawson's Creek* star was the day she purchased a copy of a *TV Guide* that featured a small cover photo of the cast. "It was funny. I handed it over to the guy behind the counter and as he handed it back he kind of looked at it and then looked back at me. He's like, 'Ummmm?' He didn't say anything else, just 'Ummmm?' So I guess you could say I've had a grunt of recognition," she told *TV Hits*.

Since the show started airing, Michelle has found herself on the cover of numerous magazines — including *TV Guide* again, which issued a *Dawson's Creek* collector's series of four covers, each featuring a different star from the show. For Michelle and her costars, fame has been a very surreal experience. "It's been such a barrage of press that I don't think we have any choice but to become used to it," she told *Seventeen*. "How do you prepare yourself for something like that? They don't give you a guidebook or anything," she mused. "It's really just a day-by-day thing. Just take things as they come and don't let yourself get too caught up in it all." Michelle thought for a moment and then laughed. "You mean, I'm going to have to put on makeup each time I go out?"

Time Out

Despite her character's glamorous image, Michelle is much more laid-back in real life. Because she wears so much makeup for the show, she prefers to keep it to the basics when she's not at work — just powder, a trace of lipstick, and a hint of mascara. She barely recognizes herself when she's made up as Jen! "When I look in the mirror after they've done my hair and makeup, it doesn't look like the same person I know. It's so unreal," she admitted to *Teen*.

Likewise, when it comes to fashion Michelle is much more interested in comfort than trendiness. "I love simple, tailored clothes, but I have to feel good in them," she told *Teen*. "I'm most comfortable in whatever I'm wearing when I wake up. I love pajamas!"

A proud new home owner, Michelle likes to spend her free time at her new digs. "I lead a really sheltered life. I like to hole up in my house with a couple of books and lay low," she said to *TV Hits*. She doesn't expect sudden fame on *Dawson's Creek* to drastically change her life. "When you hear all these things about how your life's going to change, there's no way you can prepare for that, except to stay who you are and stay grounded."

Michelle keeps in shape with a sport that's rapidly gaining more and more popularity with girls — boxing! In fact, as a child she frequently entertained a fantasy of becoming the first female heavyweight champion of the world. These days, she mixes up her punches and jabs with a bit of roadwork. "I try to run four to five miles in the Hollywood Hills, but it's hard after working all day," she revealed in *Teen*.

As for guys, Michelle really hasn't had much time for romance. "It's been a while since I've been on a date," she confessed to a teen magazine. "I barely have enough time to sleep. It's been so crazy." For right now, she's satisfied to be doing good work without having to worry about the demands of a romantic relationship. "I don't know how I would fit a boyfriend into my life anyway. I work all the time," she told *YM*. "When you're seventeen, I think it's better to be on your own. I'd rather be able to figure out who I am without having a guy influence my self-image." Sounds a lot like something Jen would say!

6
Raves and Waves

The first episode of *Dawson's Creek* hit the airwaves on January 13, 1998, and the buzz was immediate. Thanks, in part, to a widespread media campaign, including commercials and giant full-color billboards of the cast, people tuned in. In fact, when almost five million households turned on the show for the premiere episode, it looked like the three-year-old network finally had a genuine winner! *Dawson's Creek* immediately became the WB's hottest show, even beating its Tuesday night lead-in, the hit *Buffy the Vampire Slayer*! By its third week on the air, more teenagers were watching *Dawson's Creek* than any other show except for NBC's *Seinfeld*.

Keeping Their Cool

With the exception of Katie, who was in Vancouver, Canada, beginning to film her second feature film, *Disturbing Behavior*, the rest of the cast was in New Orleans promoting the show to the media and WB affiliates the day the first episode aired. Adjusting to the culture shock of finding themselves in the middle of a publicity feeding frenzy after the relative quiet of North Carolina, the cast tried their best to keep it all in perspective. "We're the new kids on the block," said Josh, the most media savvy star of the gang, during an online interview with Ultimate TV. "Personally I don't feel any pressure, because we're done already [filming the season], so it's out of my hands now."

Michelle, too, tried to take a philosophical approach to sudden fame. "I'm not sure if I should be excited, nervous, or just terrified. It's really surreal," she told *TV Hits*. "You know it's kind of dangerous to get caught up in the hype of a show and [believe] what people are saying because most of it's just hearsay. But what it all comes down to is what actually happens. I think that we've all tried to immunize ourselves against all the hype because it really can be destructive . . . I wasn't prepared for this or expecting the publicity to be so intense. It's a little overwhelming, but I'll take a deep breath and keep going."

Although her character tends to be a little secretive on *Dawson's Creek*, the real Michelle met the press with a sweet blend of good humor and honesty. "My publicity people have been really good. I've made a few faux pas, things that I really shouldn't have said that just came out, and I've been reprimanded," she told *TV Hits*. "But usually they're just like, 'Oh, say what you want.'"

James, who received the most blinding attention, both from fans and the media, prides himself on being an "actor's actor" — one who cares more about the work than the fame. "As an actor, my main responsibility is simply to show up to work on time and be prepared," he told E! online. "I can't afford to worry about the whole ratings game. It's not my job, and I really can't do anything about it."

The Raves

TV Guide gushed, "With Williamson's dead-on ear for Gen-X speak and a knack for creating solid characters, this hour is prime time's closest thing to a contemporary *Catcher in the Rye.*" Such a comparison to the most classic and revered teen angst novel of all time was a pretty heavy compliment indeed! But it didn't just end there.

All across the country, the critics started making more noise that sounded like music to the cast's and producers' ears. "It's extraordinarily rare when a new series comes along and screams 'hit' from its opening scene," wrote TV reporter Tom Jicha in Florida's *Sun-Sentinel.* "It's unprecedented for such a show to be on a second-tier network, such as the WB. But *Dawson's Creek* fits this bill."

"The new WB soap-with-smarts is going to be catnip for the Clearasil set, as achingly good-looking young actors combine with the sensibility of writer Kevin Williamson," read the prediction from the *Atlanta Journal-Constitution.*

"It's a show that even adults can like. We were all fifteen once. . . . *Dawson's Creek* doesn't talk down to its audience. . . . [It's] TV's best shot at portraying a sensitive, intelligent person growing up," opined Marvin Kitman in New York's *Newsday.*

And the reviewers were equally impressed with the *Dawson's Creek* cast.

The Hollywood Reporter called *Dawson's Creek* "a lively . . . and smart series. The particular appeal lies in the central cast, which contains young, bright break-out talent (all four)."

"Michelle Williams sizzles as Dawson's bad-girl love interest. But [Joshua] Jackson is the cast standout as audacious Pacey, who looks naive but is quite cunning," noted Kinney Littlefield in the *Orange County Register*.

"The acting is great," crowed New York's *Newsday*. "Dawson Leery, the fifteen-year-old central character, played by James Van Der Beek, is superb."

"[Katie] Holmes — the show's real center — is so perfect that you find yourself wondering why Winona Ryder hasn't just shrugged and gone into real estate," praised a writer from New York's hip *Village Voice*. National newspaper *USA Today* chose Katie for a short profile in their "Best Bet for Stardom" column, while *LA Weekly* said, "The players are talented all; any one would look fine in a poster on your bedroom wall."

In fact, the cast's girls got a head start in

the pinup category, with Katie on the cover of *Seventeen* magazine and Michelle's swank pose on *YM*'s special prom issue.

Out in cyberspace, bulletin boards buzzed with new fans of the show critiquing who's cuter, James or Josh? Other folks began a running debate over whether Dawson and Joey should remain "just friends" or move on to something more romantic. Fans of Josh, who'd been loyal since his days as a Mighty Duck, opened up new online shrines to their favorite *Dawson's Creek* guy. In fact, new Web sites detailing the biographies of James, Katie, Michelle, and Josh sprang up, literally everywhere overnight.

The Waves!

But not everyone loved *Dawson's Creek*. *People* magazine sent the show to early detention with a C+ on its report card in its weekly TV review column. *Entertainment Weekly* whined, "It's *My So-Called Life* without the life." However, the most constant refrain heard from grouchy critics across the land was that the kids of *Dawson's Creek* just don't speak like or share the same concerns as real teens.

"They look like college students, they talk like doctoral candidates (in popular culture), but they're just starting tenth grade," whined *People* magazine reviewer Terry Kelleher. "Attractive as well as articulate, all these high schoolers qualify for some sort of advanced placement. They're easy to watch, just a little hard to believe."

Carped *Entertainment Weekly* TV reviewer Ken Tucker, "Tone is a distinct problem in this show. . . . All the knowing pop-culture self-consciousness that has made Williamson's horror flicks so refreshing too often proves a didactic drag here."

TV writer Howard Rosenberg complained in the *LA Times* that the cast too often speaks in "pseudo-hip dialogue that reads great on a word processor but is foreign to the average American."

Go, Team!

Fortunately, the question of whether *Dawson's Creek* was representative of real teenagers' language and worries was something that writer Kevin Williamson and the cast were completely prepared to address. In fact, before the show had even aired, James, Josh,

89

Katie, Michelle, and Kevin met the press at the annual Television Critics' Association conference in Pasadena, California, to tell them what they thought about the controversy.

"I have heard that criticism and at first it was very surprising to me. [Their language is] a little elevated in terms of their actual age, and they do speak in a way that maybe fifteen-year-olds don't. It depends on which fifteen-year-olds you're talking to," Kevin told the gathering of reporters. "We've lived through the whole self-help psychobabble of the eighties, and I think that these kids reflect growing up during that time."

"Not every fifteen-year-old is as eloquent as Joey," said Katie, defending her character in *Teen People*, "but a lot of them are."

James rang in with an interview in *Newsday* suggesting that the way things are said on *Dawson's Creek* is not as important as *what* is said. "There are definitely kids who speak that way and who think that way. And while the dialogue isn't necessarily representative of the way every kid speaks, it's absolutely representative of how every kid feels, which I think is much more important.

"What sets [*Dawson's Creek*] apart and makes it a little bit different," he continues, "is that these characters are able to process these emotions they're going through and actually verbalize them in a way that not everyone is able to. And I think that makes it more interesting, and I think that allows us to do a lot more."

"Teens want to be seen as witty and smart and sort of, you know, in control," added Kevin in *Newsday*.

"I didn't have access to intelligent dialogue when I was a kid," said Michelle in *USA Today*. "But I wish I could have expressed my feelings this way. These issues and topics are really prevalent. Why not talk about it?"

For his part, Joshua praised the show for its language, subject matter, and the grace to let its audience think for itself. "When you start making decisions and moral judgment and preaching to your audience, you're actually insulting them," he said to *Teen Machine*. "You're saying you are smarter than they are and that you know all the right answers. Teenagers are smart enough to figure a lot out for themselves."

Katie adds in a *Newsweek* article, "It gives it a kind of a nice tone when we're analyzing and we're using big words, but at the same time we're doing the same stupid things that everybody does."

In the *New York Post*, producer Paul Stupin chimed in, "Even though [the *Dawson's Creek* characters] speak like adults, the issues they are dealing with are indicative of the teenage years and the highs and lows of growing up."

Michelle, too, defended the right for teenagers to hear the real deal. "I always imagined that some controversy would arise," she confided to *TV Hits*. "But the issues that we deal with, while they're called controversial, really are true-to-life, and they exist. And every teenager, regardless of where they live, their social standing, their class — everyone is going to be going through or feeling these emotions, so why not put it out in the open and give them some basis to go on?"

In the end, the controversy only helped *Dawson's Creek* become the most talked about show in America and the rising star of the 1998 winter TV season.

Chapter 7

Just the Facts

James's Fact File

Birth Date: March 8, 1977
Hometown: Cheshire, Connecticut
Eye and Hair Color: Blue and blond
Height: 6'
Family: James's parents are Jim and Melinda. He has a younger brother, Jared, 18, and sister, Juliana, 16.
Nicknames: Beek and Baby James
School Status: James spent two years at Drew University, where he majored in English with a minor in sociology.
Directors He'd Love to Work With: Steven Spielberg — how *very* Dawson — and Oliver Stone
First Movie He Ever Saw: *E.T.*

First Concert Attended: Green Day
Fantasy Role: Anakin Skywalker in the new *Star Wars* prequels
Worst Job Ever: "Mowing my neighbor's very steep lawn in the dead of summer when I was seventeen."

His Favorites:
Movie: *The Shawshank Redemption*
Color: Blue
Teams: New York Yankees (baseball), New Jersey Devils (hockey)
Actors: Marlon Brandon, Tom Hanks, Tim Robbins
Book: *Portrait of the Artist as a Young Man* by James Joyce
Treat: Vanilla ice cream
City: New York

His Credits:
Films:
Harvest (1998)
I Love You . . . I Love You Not (1996)
Angus (1995)

Television:
Dawson's Creek
Clarissa Explains It All (guest appearance)
The Red Booth (ABC After-school Special)

Off-Broadway Theater:
My Marriage to Ernest Borgnine
Finding the Sun

Theater:
Shenandoah

Katie's Fact File

Birth Date: December 18, 1978
Hometown: Toledo, Ohio
Eye and Hair Color: Brown and brown
Height: 5' 8"
Family: Dad's an attorney; Mom's a home-maker. Katie has three older sisters and an older brother.
Worst Habit: "I drink too much coffee."
Directors She'd Love to Work With: Oliver Stone, Ron Howard, Woody Allen
First Movie She Ever Saw: *E.T.*
First Concert Attended: Whitney Houston
Fantasy Role: Sydney in *Scream 3*
Worst Job Ever: "Mowing the neighbor's lawn for twenty dollars when I was fourteen. It was so hot and sticky."
Secret Desire: To do a period movie dressed in elaborate costumes

Her Favorites:
Movie: *My Best Friend's Wedding*
Music: Dave Matthews Band, Natalie Merchant, Jewel
Actors: Jodie Foster, Julia Roberts, Tom Hanks, Meg Ryan
Hobbies: Shopping, dancing, watching basketball

Her Credits:
Films:
Go! (1999)
Killing Mrs. Tingle (1998)
Disturbing Behavior (1998)
The Ice Storm (1997)

Television:
Dawson's Creek

Josh's Fact File

Birth Date: June 11, 1978
Hometown: Vancouver, Canada
Eye and Hair Color: Blue and brown
Height: 6'
Family: Mom, Fiona, is a casting director. Josh has a younger sister, Aisleegh.
Nickname: Jackson

Pets: Shumba, a dog, and Saorse, a turtle

Car: Chevy Tahoe

Prized Possession: A silver pocket watch

Acting Influences: "My mother, my life, and the people around me."

Directors He'd Love to Work With: "Anyone who'll hire me."

First Movie He Ever Saw: *E.T.*

First Concert Attended: The Bee Gees at age four

Fantasy Role: David Balfour, a Charles Dickens character from the book of the same name

Worst Habit: Josh is a self-admitted slob.

His Favorites:

Movie: *Good Will Hunting*

Sports: Hockey and football

CD: Common Sense's *Resurrection*

Actors: Sean Connery, Matt Damon, Samuel L. Jackson

Book: *Lord of the Rings* by J.R.R. Tolkien

Vacation spot: Ireland

His Credits:

Films:

Apt Pupil (1998)

Wild River (1998)

Scream 2 (1997)
D3: The Mighty Ducks (1996)
Magic in the Water (1995)
D2: The Mighty Ducks (1994)
Andre (1994)
Digger (1993)
The Mighty Ducks (1992)
Crooked Hearts (1991)

Cable TV Movies:
Robin of Locksley (1996)
Ronnie and Julie (1996)

Television:
Dawson's Creek
Outer Limits (guest appearance)

Michelle's Fact File

Birth Date: September 9, 1980
Hometown: Kalispell, Montana and San Diego, California
Family: Mom is Carla, Dad is Harry, and Michelle has a younger sister, Paige.
First Movie She Ever Saw: *E.T.*
First Concert Attended: Neil Diamond
Fantasy Role: Gertrude from the Hermann Hesse book of the same name.

Worst Job Ever: "Working on the movie *Timemaster*. It was so awful. We turn the *M* upside down and call it *TimeWaster*. Outside of the business, during a dry spell, I scooped ice cream at the county fair, and I ate more than I sold. Making a cone is difficult, and I lost so many scoops into the chocolate swirl."

Her Favorites:

Actor: Katharine Hepburn

Book: *Notes from the Underground* by Fyodor Dostoyevsky

Authors: Hermann Hesse, Fyodor Dostoyevsky, Kurt Vonnegut

Treat: Häagen-Daz chocolate ice cream, chocolate brownies

Hobbies: Boxing, reading

Her Credits:

Films:

A Thousand Acres (1997)

Species (1995)

Timemaster (1995)

Lassie (1994)

TV Movies:

A Mother's Justice

Killing Mr. Griffin

Television:
Dawson's Creek
Home Improvement (guest appearance)
Step By Step (guest appearance)

100 *Dawson's Creek* Fast Facts

1. Josh Jackson admits to not taking school very seriously when he was fifteen. "I got kicked out of high school twice," he told *YM* magazine, "once for attitude and once for lack of attendance."

2. Series creator Kevin Williamson says that the cast is handling success so well that a frequent joke on the set is which one of them will become the first to get a star attitude. "We have all our cards on Dawson because it's his creek!" he joked to E! online.

3. Everyone agrees that Joshua Jackson has the personality closest to the character he plays. "I'm the class clown," he told *Seventeen*.

4. One of the first films to be lensed in Wilmington was the 1984 horror flick *Firestarter*, which starred a very young Drew Barrymore.

5.   Katie's parents gave all five of their children piano lessons.

6.   James's favorite TV show — not counting *Dawson's Creek* — is *Monday Night Football*.

7.   Michelle used to have a fantasy about becoming the first female heavyweight champion of the world.

8.   Kevin describes *Dawson's Creek* as "*Northern Exposure* meets *My So-Called Life.*"

9.   The producers of *Dawson's Creek* originally brought the idea for the series to the Fox TV network. Fox turned the series down because they thought it was too similar to *Party of Five*.

10.   At her very first professional audition, Katie landed the role of Libbets Casey in the 1997 movie *The Ice Storm*.

11.   The producers wanted to use Alanis Morissette's hit song "Hand in My Pocket" as the opening theme of *Dawson's Creek*, but she refused to license her tune. Luckily, Paula Cole had no such objection! Her "I Don't Want to Wait" is the show's theme song.

12.   Although *The Mighty Ducks* film tril-

ogy was a comedy, Joshua played Charlie, the most serious ice hockey player on the team. "I've been in comedies, but I've never *done* comedy," he told *Tiger Beat*.

13. James called playwright Edward Albee, who cast James in his off-Broadway play *Finding the Sun*, "the most brilliant man I've ever met."

14. Katie would love to play a darker character in a future project. She'll probably have her chance — she plays rebellious teens in both *Disturbing Behavior* and *Go!*

15. Kevin Williamson had a letter hand-delivered to director Steven Spielberg asking his permission to use his name and references to his movies in the pilot episode of *Dawson's Creek*. "Rumor has it he saw the first episode and loved it," said James to E! "He also gave his blessing to use his name and image."

16. *YM* printed James' take on Dawson — "He's a tragically nice guy — and so am I."

17. Josh is particularly happy to be involved in a show that doesn't stress a "message." "Teenagers are smart

enough to figure out a lot for themselves," he told *Tiger Beat*. "We go under the assumption that the audience can make up their own minds about the situations that arise on the show."

18. Michelle told *Seventeen* magazine that when she's living in North Carolina she misses "being able to grocery shop at three in the morning." Apparently, she did that in L.A.!

19. In the movie *Angus*, James played the obnoxious football player boyfriend of *Jurassic Park* star Ariana Richards.

20. After he graduated from high school, Josh took some time off from acting to travel through Europe. His favorite country was Ireland.

21. How romantic is James? Once, he told *YM*, he prepared a nighttime picnic for his girlfriend on a city rooftop. "We just watched the stars."

22. Katie's hometown best friend plays for her school's basketball team. When Katie is in Ohio she tries to show up to cheer her friend on to victory.

23. Michelle was miffed when she saw the final version of the scene when Jen first meets Dawson and the gang on

103

the dock. She thought her skirt looked much too short!

24. As a kid, Katie attempted to play softball and basketball, but she wasn't very good at either. That's why she tried acting.

25. Joshua appeared on an episode of *Outer Limits* that also starred *Small Soldiers'* Kirsten Dunst.

26. Kevin says that one of the influences for *Dawson's Creek* was a TV show he enjoyed as a kid. It was called *James at 15* and it ran on TV from October 27, 1977 to July 27, 1978.

27. Great songs from Sheryl Crow, the Cardigans, No Doubt, Paula Cole, Third Eye Blind, and Jewel can be heard during each episode of *Dawson's Creek*.

28. Through the relationship of Dawson and Joey, Kevin is getting a chance to relive some of the things that happened between him and his best friend, Fanny. "There are some things I said to Fanny as that boy that I wish I hadn't," he told the *Philadelphia Daily News*. "And now I get to go back and say them, and then to apologize for them."

29. Michelle hated her high school in San Diego. She'd spend most lunch hours hiding in the girls' room. By home schooling and working with a tutor, she was able to graduate early, at age fifteen.

30. Although Joey rows her boat to Dawson's house, Katie doesn't have to actually row. The boat is rigged with a rope on the bottom that the crew pulls to make it look like Katie is really moving the boat all on her own.

31. Michelle avoids watching episodes of the show because she's hypercritical of her performance. Katie, however, enjoys watching the show because she's always curious to see which shot the director used.

32. Although Josh sometimes suggests a different way for Pacey to say a line, he doesn't feel it's his place to offer plot twists to the show's writers. "I'm nineteen and I have no experience producing or writing a TV show, so I wouldn't know what I'm talking about," he reasoned.

33. Katie likes to run three or four miles a couple of times a week. She says that

it really helps clear her head from all the tension and stress of being on the set.

34. Josh starred in the Showtime cable movie *Robin of Locksley* along with *Casper* actor Devon Sawa. In this update of the legend of Robin Hood, Josh plays John Prince Jr., the bad guy!

35. Michelle told *TV Hits* that being on *Dawson's Creek* hasn't changed her life much, except that now, "I have to go buy nice dresses." She's still trying to get used to seeing her own face on those gigantic *Dawson's Creek* billboards.

36. James was the last core member of the *Dawson's Creek* foursome to be cast. He flew down to North Carolina to start filming the pilot just three days after snagging the role.

37. Kevin Williamson was named one of the "100 Most Creative People in Entertainment" in 1997 by *Entertainment Weekly*. Among his upcoming features is a black comedy called *Killing Mrs. Tingle*, which is Kevin's revenge on a former teacher who once said he had no talent.

38. *Teen People* held an online poll to find out whether *Dawson's Creek*'s viewers like Jen or Joey more. Sorry, Jennifer, Joey won!

39. Michelle, like Jen, isn't necessarily looking for love. "I'm still figuring out who I am," she said in a recent interview, "so a steady boy isn't what I want right now. Besides, I wouldn't know where to find the time."

40. Kevin is trying to write a guest-starring role for Sarah Michelle Gellar, star of *Buffy the Vampire Slayer*, in a future episode of *Dawson's Creek*. Because she was killed in both Kevin's *I Know What You Did Last Summer* and *Scream 2*, she would really like her character to die on *Dawson's Creek*, too.

41. Katie is a fan of '70s rock singer Janis Joplin.

42. Josh admits that he's not so smooth with girls. "I'd like to be romantic," he confessed to a reporter, "but generally, I'm too oblivious."

43. Although there are a number of Internet sites dedicated to *Dawson's Creek*, don't expect to meet Michelle visiting them. Computers "are all foreign con-

traptions to me," she told *TV Hits*. "I can't even type my name."

44. James has tried to steel himself for stardom. "I'd like to think I'm completely ready, but I have no idea what to expect," he confessed in an interview.

45. Katie's set trailer is painted in shades of blue. The color has a calming effect on her.

46. Josh once sang with the San Francisco Boys' Chorus, although today the only singing he does is in the shower!

47. Michelle, who's single, spent Valentine's Day 1998 watching romantic movies with some friends and eating Häagen-Daz chocolate ice cream. It's her favorite treat next to chocolate brownies.

48. Katie admits that in high school she was never one of those girls who got all the guys. Of course, since she attended an all-girls school, there weren't a ton of cute boys around, either.

49. Both Michelle and Katie have starred in projects with fellow teen actor Nick Stahl. Katie filmed *Disturbing Behavior* with him and *Second Noah*'s James

Marsden, while Michelle and Nick appeared in a TV movie called *A Mother's Justice*.

50. Josh Jackson once told a teen magazine that the only things he looks for in a girlfriend are "teeth and a pulse!" However, he would also like to meet someone nice who appreciates his wacky sense of humor.

51. Although he's played the bully in two movies — *Angus* and *I Love You . . . I Love You Not* — James admits that during his middle school years, he was the one who got picked on by the bigger guys.

52. Katie has been accepted to Columbia University in New York City. She's deferred her enrollment but definitely plans to go back to school one day, possibly as an English major.

53. Kevin sent his old friend Fanny — who's the real-life inspiration for the character Joey — an early video of the *Dawson's Creek* pilot. She loved it!

54. Two first-season episodes of *Dawson's Creek* were satires — one was a spoof of *The Breakfast Club* and one parodied Kevin's own *Scream*. These episodes

were so popular among the cast and *Dawson's Creek* viewers that they'll be doing more parodies next season.

55. Josh is the "cast clown." When someone has to be really serious, or even cry in a scene, trust Josh to be just out of camera range — mooning his castmate!

56. James's dad played minor league baseball with the Los Angeles Dodgers. At one time, James assumed he'd follow in his father's footsteps and play ball for a living, too.

57. At an international modeling and talent convention in New York, Katie was discovered by her manager. He convinced her to try out for *The Ice Storm*, her first professional job!

58. Although Josh says it's a compliment to be compared with *My So-Called Life*, he thinks the characters on *Dawson's Creek* are happier and more secure than Angela Chase and her friends.

59. Although Joey's had romantic thoughts about Dawson, Katie confesses she's never thought about James — or any of her other costars — as anything but a friend!

60. At thirteen, James sustained a minor concussion that forced him to sit out the football season. So he tried out for the school play and landed the lead role!

61. Josh recently leased a new car. It's a Chevy Tahoe.

62. It's hard to believe, but *Dawson's Creek* is only Katie's second professional acting job ever.

63. In 1991, James made his first TV appearance on Nickelodeon's *Clarissa Explains It All*. He played a character named Paulie.

64. Even though Michelle's the youngest cast member, she insists she has "a past."

65. To pass the time on the set of *Dawson's Creek*, James has been teaching himself to play guitar. He also writes in his journal.

66. Katie played Lola in her high school's production of the musical *Damn Yankees*. She even postponed her second *Dawson's Creek* audition to make sure she was at the play's opening night.

67. When Katie goes home to be with her friends and family in Toledo, she loves to go to coffeehouses and then rent videos.

68. Unlike Dawson, James says he's never up early enough in the morning to watch the *Today Show*.

69. Michelle, who's a natural blond, is thinking about going brunette just to try something different.

70. Josh is very proud of his Irish heritage. In fact, he named his redheaded turtle Saorse, which is the Irish word for "freedom."

71. Katie graduated from her all-girls high school with a 3.8 grade point average.

72. Like Dawson, Kevin was obsessed with movies. As a teenager, he convinced his school librarian to order a subscription to the movie industry trade publication *Variety*.

73. How has stardom changed James's life? "I can afford to eat now," he joked on the Ultimate TV Web site.

74. Josh's favorite kinds of music are rap, hip-hop, jazz, and blues.

75. Katie took ballet and jazz dance lessons as a child.

76. When the cast has time off, they like

to make a road trip to nearby Wrightsville Beach for a little bit of fun in the sun.

77. Don't expect to meet James online, either. He doesn't have a computer right now.

78. Josh says that one of the things he hates most is getting water up his nose.

79. Although he doesn't do gymnastics much anymore, James likes to try to get to the gym to maintain his flexibility.

80. Josh's dog, Shumba, appears in the J. Crew winter 1998 catalogue along with the rest of the *Dawson's Creek* cast.

81. Michelle says that, while she wouldn't dress like Jen in real life, she doesn't mind wearing most of her character's clothes.

82. Josh landed his first professional job in a commercial promoting tourism in British Columbia.

83. Kevin refers to his characters as "my kids."

84. Like Joey, Katie's a tomboy. She'll take sneakers and jeans over high heels and gowns any day!

85. James is often compared to other actors. *USA Today* called him a "Matthew McConaughey look-alike," while *Entertainment Weekly* dubbed him "Ethan Hawke with better hygiene."

86. Critics and TV writers are already calling Katie the break-out star of *Dawson's Creek*. She spent her winter hiatus filming the movies *Disturbing Behavior*, *Killing Mrs. Tingle*, and *Go!*

87. Michelle did a movie over the winter break, too. She filmed *Halloween: H20*, which also starred Josh Hartnett and Joseph Gordon-Levitt.

88. If acting didn't work out for him, James might have become a middle school teacher.

89. If Michelle had her way, she insists she'd never leave her house. This self-confessed homebody loves nothing better than curling up with a cup of hot chocolate and a good video — or better, a good book.

90. Katie's a bit of a shopaholic. Before she started making her own money, her older brother and sisters used to take pity and drop her some cash for new clothes.

91. In 1997, Joshua starred in a cable TV remake of the classic love story *Romeo and Juliet*, called *Ronnie and Julie*.

92. Michelle likes to write her innermost thoughts in a journal.

93. Josh says, "If Hollywood is a state of mind, then I'm an ignorant man." As you might guess, this native of Vancouver, Canada, isn't moving to Los Angeles anytime soon.

94. Katie says that if she were one of the original Brat Pack, she'd be Molly Ringwald, while Josh thinks he'd be fellow *Mighty Ducks* veteran Emilio Estevez.

95. Josh briefly considered going to college and studying architecture or archaeology. Now he's thinking he'd like to study English or philosophy. He'd definitely like to get a degree after his time on *Dawson's Creek* is over.

96. The entire cast did an extreme fashion layout in *YM* magazine — *very* cool!

97. Before he became a successful screenwriter, Kevin was an out-of-work actor and an assistant to a music video director.

98. Call him Mr. Popularity: When James attended the private high school Cheshire Academy, he went to four proms!

99. Katie says her worst vice is drinking too much coffee.

100. *Dawson's Creek* is a real place located near the town of New Bern, North Carolina, about two hours away from where the series is filmed.

8

It's All in the Stars

To find out what's going on at *Dawson's Creek*, all you have to do is turn on your TV once a week. But for an all-in-fun peek at the forces shaping James's, Katie's, Joshua's, and Michelle's personalities, just look at their zodiac signs!

James: A Dreamy Pisces

James's Star Chart
Birth Date: March 8
Astrological Sign: Pisces
Pisces Symbol: The Fish
Pisces Element: Water
Pisces Gems: Amethyst and Emerald

Pisces Flower: Water lily

Positive Pisces Traits: Creative, easygoing, artistic, tolerant, charming, intuitive, empathetic, generous, curious

Negative Pisces Traits: Oversensitive, secretive, lazy, impractical, solitary, easily depressed

James's Pisces Personality

It's funny that James is a Pisces in real life, because the starry-eyed fish would almost certainly be the zodiac sign of his character, Dawson Leery, who often lives in a fantasy world of his own. People born under the sign of Pisces love to while away the hours dreaming. They have the most active imaginations of any zodiac sign and often live in a rose-colored world of their own making. James admits that one of the reasons he relates to Dawson is that they both had very positive dreams and ambitions from a very young age.

Professionally, Pisceans are often very creative and are drawn toward a career in the arts. Piscean actors, in fact, are naturally attracted to the theater, where they can live out their dreams in each performance. In true Piscean fashion, James spent the earliest part of his career on the New York stage and has often said that he'd like to return to the theater someday.

Pisceans are usually very even-tempered people who rarely lose their cool and are very tolerant of others' peculiarities. They're almost never greedy. Material possessions can't compare with the fabulous flights of fancy going on in the mind of the creative Pisces. As long as this placid fish has just enough possessions to be warm and comfortable, he's very happy.

James in Love

So what does James's star sign reveal about his feelings on love? Well, any girl who gets involved with a Pisces had better like romance, because there are few signs more capable of heartfelt romantic gestures than the dreamy fish. Pisceans live and breathe romance! They can find it anywhere — a spot of moonlight reflected off a shop window can make them swoon. Pisceans live in a romantic world of dreams, illusions, and grand fantasies, and if you're the kind of girl who appreciates tales of castles in the air, then a Pisces like James is for you.

119

A guy born under the sign of Pisces is also one of those rare types who is a great listener. He has a sympathetic ear for everyone, from his male buddies to his mom to a stranger in the checkout line of the grocery store. He's not the type to pass judgment on others, either, no matter how terrible their secrets. Pisceans are also very good at keeping secrets — if you ask a Pisces to keep something quiet, you can be sure you won't find your business blabbed on the evening news. These traits give Pisces a wealth of friends of both sexes, so if you're the jealous type, be prepared to bite your tongue. Don't blame him — a Pisces like James just can't help drawing others into his fantastic dreamworld!

There's not much need for jealousy, however. Pisces are as loyal as they are romantic. Although there can be moments of exasperation when you'd like nothing better than to shake him out of his fantasy world, it's easier just to give in and swim along with the tide yourself. If you can appreciate the things in life that money can't buy, then a Pisces guy like James is all you've ever dreamed of!

Katie: Sagittarius, the Outgoing Archer

Katie's Star Chart

Birth Date: December 18
Astrological Sign: Sagittarius
Sagittarius Symbol: The Archer
Sagittarius Element: Fire
Sagittarius Gem: Topaz
Sagittarius Flower: Carnation
Positive Sagittarius Traits: Friendly, direct, honest, warm, generous, intelligent, talkative, optimistic
Negative Sagittarius Traits: Tactless, clumsy, rebellious, a blabbermouth

Katie's Sagittarius Personality

The entertainment industry is full of people like Katie, who were born under the sign of Sagittarius, the Archer. Perhaps it is because most Sagittarians have really great memories, so learning dialogue is a snap. Most Archers are also outgoing, talkative, and friendly, too. Like Katie, they enjoy being around others and inspire great loyalty in their friends with their warm and generous personalities.

People born under the sign of Sagittarius can be honest to a fault. That's because they just can't tell a believable lie. They're also direct and blunt, so if you ask a Sagittarius for her opinion, be sure you're ready to hear the unadorned truth — even if it hurts! But it's not like she's being mean. Katie and her fellow Archers never try to hurt anyone's feelings, they just can't seem to accurately measure how much truth others really need to hear. Another possible difficulty is that they're not the best at keeping secrets. It's that truth problem again that makes them say exactly what just pops into their minds — even if it's your deep and dark secret! Only tell a Sagittarius the things you don't mind someone else hearing.

People born under the sign of Sagittarius are generally happy with their lives and their friends. They tend to love animals, parties, and being outdoors. (Katie's favorite exercise is going for a run, no matter how cold the weather.)

Katie in Love

Whether it's love or just good friendship, Katie and her fellow Sagittarians like to have people around who respect their private space. They don't mind living alone with maybe just a couple of pets. Although they're warm and friendly to most everyone, Sagittarius people are very independent and enjoy spending time by themselves.

Sagittarians never hide what they're feeling. The minute a thought occurs to them, they express it. Honest Sagittarius souls don't believe in playing silly games in relationships. She'll tell you exactly what she thinks of you, whether you ask her or not. She's drawn to people who have firm opinions but who aren't bossy. As a Fire sign, Sagittarians can have explosive tempers. But on the whole, Katie and the other people born under her sign make fun, lively, and outgoing friends.

Joshua: The Wacky Gemini

Joshua's Star Chart
Birth Date: June 11
Astrological Sign: Gemini
Gemini Symbol: The Twins
Gemini Element: Air
Gemini Gem: Aquamarine
Gemini Flower: Lily-of-the-Valley
Positive Gemini Traits: Fun, energetic, clever, witty, charming, honest
Negative Gemini Traits: Unpredictable, easily sidetracked, impatient, flaky

Josh's Gemini Personality

Geminis like Josh can talk to anyone about anything. They have a talent for words. They're often fast talkers and fast thinkers who can disarm you with their free-spirited charm. Their quick minds are always ready with a wisecrack or a witty remark — just like Josh *and* his *Dawson's Creek* character, Pacey! Gemini people are often talented in multiple areas. They have no problem juggling many different things at once.

The symbol for Gemini is the twins; this symbol reflects the unpredictable nature of Geminis. Geminis tend to have a very short attention span, so even if they have every intention of doing something, they easily get pulled off course. Their actions and opinions are always surprising and are constantly changing. Ask a Gemini for an opinion and he'll gladly tell you what he thinks, but if you ask him the same question a day or an hour later, don't be surprised if he's totally reversed his thoughts! He's not lying — it's just that he's changed his mind!

Although Geminis love to talk, they prefer not to focus on themselves. It's not that they're secretive, exactly. They're just uncomfortable sharing their deepest emotions with others. Perhaps it's because the twin person-

alities cause a Gemini to never feel the same
way or think the same thoughts for very long!

Josh in Love

In matters of the heart, Geminis like Josh
are just as restless and unpredictable as they
are in every other part of their life. He can be
the perfect guy one day — romantic, witty,
fun — and then the next, he's distant, restless,
and moody. It's the other Gemini twin you're
seeing and you'd better get used to it, because
both sides are very much a part of him. It
takes a very secure person to take a Gemini's
varying personality in stride and be happy.

But Geminis can also be wonderful. They're
generous with compliments and extremely
fun to be around. At a party, Geminis are often the center of attention, telling stories and
enchanting everyone who comes within hearing range. Truthfully, he just hates being
alone. And although he enjoys the attention
of girls, a Gemini like Josh has a sense of fair-
ness that will make him always remain true.

Michelle: The Vigorous Virgo

Michelle's Star Chart
Birth Date: September 9

Astrological Sign: Virgo
Virgo Symbol: The Virgin
Virgo Element: Earth
Virgo Gem: Jade
Virgo Flower: Hyacinth
Positive Virgo Traits: Perfectionist, sincere, dependable, neat, orderly, detail-oriented
Negative Virgo Traits: Worrywart, vain, nervous, fussy

Michelle's Virgo Personality

Virgos like Michelle are hard workers who enjoy living a very neat and tidy existence. They have really great organizational skills and never complain, even when doing the most boring, mindless jobs. Virgos get a lot of satisfaction out of a job well done. They're often practical, perceptive, and have excellent taste in everything from clothes to music. Just like their orderly living spaces, Michelle and other people born under the sign of Virgo always look clean and neat as well. You wouldn't catch most Virgos outdoors in wrinkled clothes!

Most people born under the sign of the virgin dislike large gatherings of people. Essentially, shy Virgos prefer to make friends one-on-one. They're good to their friends, too, often putting the needs of others before themselves. Although Virgos tend to be critical, it's a small relief to know that they're just as critical of themselves as they are of everyone else.

Michelle in Love

When it comes to the opposite sex, Virgos tend to be both lavishly romantic and coldly practical. She's looking for an idealized relationship and anything short of perfection simply doesn't work. Although she'll walk over mountains for the love of her life, a Virgo is also likely to quickly break off a relationship that isn't working. She's not being mean, just practical.

Virgos always want the best for their friends and loved ones. Born worriers, they can't help but care! Because they believe that no one is as orderly as they are, Virgos can be a little opinionated about the right way to do something. The most annoying thing is that they're usually right! Despite their critical ways, people born under the sign of Virgo are often kind, affectionate, generous, and faithful friends. Michelle certainly has the positive Virgo traits.

9

Predictions, Where to Write, and More!

What lies ahead for Dawson, Joey, Pacey, and Jen? How about James, Katie, Josh, and Michelle? Well, the gang will definitely be back for season two of the hit show. And chances are, avid fans of the show still won't know if Pacey will ever get a girl who appreciates him, or if Joey and Dawson belong together forever. As for Jen, there's a good chance that more interesting secrets will be coming out of her closet!

There will definitely be more movie parody episodes in the new season, because *The Breakfast Club* show was a huge favorite among *Dawson's Creek* fans and the cast as well. "It's great," Josh said of the episode, which along with "The Hurricane" is one of his favorites. They're hoping to attract some big name guest stars to the show in season two. Sarah Michelle Gellar has said she'd like to come on — possibly even as Buffy the Vampire Slayer.

Buffy might not be the only visitor to Capeside. It's possible that an episode next season could include a regular *Dawson's Creek* viewer just like you! Josh mentioned a plan to have a promotion to "win a spot" on the show.

Life Outside *Dawson's Creek*

When they weren't promoting *Dawson's Creek*, Katie, James, Michelle, and Josh had the freedom to pursue other projects during the first half of 1998. Like *Buffy*'s Sarah Michelle Gellar or *Party of Five*'s Neve Campbell, the girls of *Dawson's Creek* used their successful series as a springboard to starring roles on the silver screen.

Katie Holmes, who only had one movie on her resumé before *Dawson's Creek*, spent a busy winter filming three: *Disturbing Behavior*, *Killing Mrs. Tingle*, and *Go!*

In *Disturbing Behavior*, James Marsden, of *Second Noah* fame, plays Steve Clark, a new kid who moves to a small town where formerly rebellious teenagers are weirdly transformed into mild-mannered, upstanding citizens. With Katie's character, Rachel, a juvenile delinquent from the wrong side of town, as his tour guide, Steve begins to understand the horrific side effects of the other teenagers' reformation. It's up to him to solve the mystery before he's targeted for an attitude adjustment of his own. Expect to see a very different Katie in her *Disturbing Behavior* portrayal of wild Rachel, complete with "nose ring and everything."

Katie continues to misbehave in the film *Killing Mrs. Tingle*, where she's the ringleader of a bunch of high school students intent on murdering their most hated teacher. Written by Kevin Williamson, this horror comedy will be his directorial debut.

Finally, Katie reteams with her *Ice Storm* costar Christina Ricci in *Go!*, a film scheduled for release in early 1999. This "gritty comedy" follows the adventures of a bunch of actors and assorted misfits who meet in Los Angeles and then move on to Las Vegas.

Katie's not the only *Dawson's Creek* cast member willing to try new roles. After settling into her very first home high in the Hollywood Hills, Michelle signed on to star in the much-anticipated sequel to the *Halloween* film series. Twenty years after she became the first survivor of deranged killer Michael Myer's attacks, Jamie Lee Curtis returns to the screen as Laurie Strode in *Halloween: H20*. Jamie will be the mom of a teenaged son played by *Cracker*'s Josh Hartnett. Michelle and *Third Rock from the Sun*'s Joseph Gordon-Levitt play teens ready to match wits with the ultimate evil. *Halloween: H20* should give scary-movie fans plenty of thrills, chills, and interesting plot twists.

James, who as Dawson was obligated to do more publicity than his cast members, found himself back in his beloved New York City by February 1998 looking for a choice opportunity to return to the theater stage. Although he's proud of his work on *Dawson's Creek* and would love to do more films, he admits that theater is and always will be his first love. "For me, filming is taking what you do on stage and trying to transfer that," he told *Tiger Beat*. "I think theater is what it's all about. I'll never leave theater."

And while Josh would never turn down a good role, he's extremely thrilled to have some time to spend with his family and friends in Vancouver. "My free time is pretty much like everyone else's free time — but I don't have to work, which is cool," he told E!

No matter where they venture during their hiatus, you can be sure that Katie, James, Michelle, and Josh will be traveling back to *Dawson's Creek* come summer 1998. They're all too in love with the drama series to even start considering leaving for good. Even writer Kevin Williamson, who's swamped by many different projects, has a hard time leaving *Dawson's Creek* for long. "This is sort of my childhood come to life," he told reporters at a *Dawson's Creek* press conference. "That's what's so cool about it. That's why I'm so passionate about it and so involved with it."

On the Web

So far, Joshua Jackson is the only *Dawson's Creek* star who confesses to surfing the Internet on a regular basis, but all four cast members have gone online for chats and the occasional peek at the *Dawson's Creek* sites that have popped up. In fact, new sites dedicated to this fabulous foursome are launching every day.

"I'm going to start a Katie page," joked James during an online interview with Ultimate TV. In fact, a lot of people have already beaten him to creating unofficial Katie Holmes Web sites. As this book went to press, she was right behind Josh as the most popular *Dawson's Creek* star online. "I've already been to the 'I love Josh Jackson' page," joked James. "I like to put in comments, like, 'I think Josh is dreamy!'"

If you're looking for information, photos, or downloads of the *Dawson's Creek* cast, there's no better place to start than at the show's official sites on the World Wide Web. Produced by the gang at Ultimate TV, the WB's official *Dawson's Creek* site can be found at **www.dawsons-creek.com/** and it's chockful of really cool stuff. The Media Gallery allows visitors to access video and audio clips from *Dawson's Creek* as well as photographs. Another great feature is their music spot, where fans can check out the bands featured on episodes of the show. Want to e-mail a friend a snap from *Dawson's Creek*? Just click the postcards button to create your own. This site also includes star biographies, episode synopses, bulletin board, FAQs, games, and a chat room.

Columbia/TriStar, the producers of the series, also have their own official *Dawson's Creek* site, which has some nice interactive features. Accessed at **www.spe.sony.com/tv/shows/dawson**, this site promises live chats with the cast. It also includes weekly polls, as well as a listing of when the *Dawson's Creek* gang are appearing on TV talk shows. Finally, this site offers multiple multimedia downloads from every *Dawson's Creek* episode to date.

The Unofficial *Dawson's Creek* Web Page can be accessed at **www.geocities.com/~dawcreek/**. In addition to bios, episode guides, and sound bites, this site includes downloadable movies in both Quicktime and Real Player formats. There's a very neat archive of articles that have appeared about the series in everything from *Variety* to *Entertainment Weekly*, as well as photos from the cast's stint as models for the J. Crew catalogue. The biggest oddity available here is a downloadable message of Josh, Katie, or Michelle saying, "You've got mail," for use by people on AOL.

Further into the world of fan-created *Dawson's Creek* sites, it's worthwhile to stop by Elan's *Dawson's Creek* page, if for no other reason than to see the lovely shimmering reflection she programmed into the water around

Dawson's rowboat on the opening splash. Elan is fond of polling visitors to the site with neat questions and then posting the results. For example, in February 1998, fifty-one percent of her visitors thought Joey and Dawson should become more than just friends. This site also includes Web links, articles, message boards, and a chat room. It can be found at **members.aol.com/elanxyz**.

US Entertainment: *Dawson's Creek* A Tribute contains seventy-five photos from the show to download as well as the usual bios, episode guides, articles, links, etc. Among the video clips available for download is a television interview with James talking about his role on the show. Reach it at **www.usentertainment.com/television/drama.dawsons_creek**.

Make a Friend at the Creek, a site that can be reached at **members.xoom.com/dawsonscreek**, includes a chat room, photo gallery, a place to vote for your favorite *Dawson's Creek* characters, and some well-written opinion articles about the show by the site's authors.

Another site that shows promise is *Dawson's Creek*, a fan site by author Babygirl. It showcases lots of photos, bios, and a listing of cast members' upcoming appearances on TV. Enter this site at **www.geocities.com/southbeach/pier/4083/dawsonscreek.html**

Write to the Cast!
Want to get in touch with the cast of *Dawson's Creek* by snail mail? Well, they'd love to hear from you!
Write to:
Dawson's Creek
The WB
4000 Warner Boulevard
Burbank, CA 91522

About the Author

Angie Nichols's celebrity profiles and interviews have appeared in many national teen magazines over the past decade. She makes her home in the New York City area and never misses an episode of Dawson's Creek. *Her favorite character is Pacey!*